The Rednecks Are Coming!

WHY DO HAIRCUTS FOR REDNECKS
COST EIGHT DOLLARS?
THE CHARGE IS TWO DOLLARS PER
CORNER.

*.   LEARN THE BELLY-BOUNCING
ANSWERS TO . . .*

HOW DO YOU GET THREE REDNECKS
OFF A COUCH?
WHO ARE THE SIX MOST IMPORTANT
PEOPLE AT A REDNECK WEDDING?
WHAT IS A HILLYBILLY VACATION?
IF SIX GIRLS ARE WEARING
RAINCOATS, HOW CAN YOU TELL
WHICH ONE IS THE REDNECK?

WILD! BAWDY! DOWNRIGHT
COUNTRIFIED CRAZINESS!

REDNECKS!

FROM AMERICA'S #1 BESTSELLING
HUMORIST
LARRY WILDE

REDNECKS

LARRY WILDE

Illustrations by Ron Wing

BANTAM BOOKS
TORONTO · NEW YORK · LONDON · SYDNEY

REDNECKS

A Bantam Book / April 1984

ISBN 0-553-24106-0

Published simultaneously in the United States and Canada

Bantam Books are published by Bantam Books, Inc. Its trade-mark, consisting of the words ''Bantam Books'' and the por-trayal of a rooster, is Registered in U.S. Patent and Trademark Office and in other countries. Marca Registrada. Bantam Books, Inc., 666 Fifth Avenue, New York, New York 10103.

PRINTED IN THE UNITED STATES OF AMERICA

O   0 9 8 7 6 5 4 3 2 1

To Georgia's Billy Carter:
One of the few Americans
bold enough to actually
admit he is a redneck.

CONTENTS

INTRODUCTION

Everyday in the news we are deluged with the difficulties and problems of our country's ethnic and religious groups. Stories abound of underprivileged Puerto Ricans, put upon Poles, misunderstood Mexicans, beleaguered Blacks, intimidated Italians—the list is endless.

Yet nowhere to be found is there sympathy, compassion or understanding for the poor redneck, an abused creature in American society. The redneck is significant in numbers and can be observed in every region of the U.S. He could be your next door neighbor. Perhaps this will help you recognize him:

A redneck chews tobacco and sports a large pot belly hidden under a dirty T-shirt.

His hobbies are shooting pool, going on strike and sex. (With anyone but his wife.)

The redneck's idea of a dream vehicle is a 4-wheel drive pickup with an American flag decal on the windshield and a red-white-and-blue rifle rack in the rear window.

1

His favorite drinks are a case of Schlitz, a quart of Canadian Club and a bottle of Alka Seltzer.

His favorite foods are beer nuts . . . beef jerky . . . Velveeta cheese . . . anything between two slices of Wonder Bread.

His favorite TV shows are Monday Night Football . . . Road Runner Cartoons.

His favorite colors are Red (as in necks), White (as in socks) and Blue (as in collars.)

The last book he read was "Fun With Dick and Jane."

The redneck's ideal wife is barefoot and pregnant . . . Makes a mean Spam casserole with two kinds of canned soup . . . Keeps quiet during Monday Night Football and Road Runner Cartoons.

His ideal mistress is a woman whose husband works nights. She wears red (panties), White (lipstick) and Blue (eyeshadow).

And the redneck is a religious man. He prays to Jeezus H. Christ (only during Monday Night Football).

The term redneck is a fairly new one. The original expression meant one whose years of labor in the sun-parched fields gave him a tough, reddened neck. But with the passage of time and the redneck participation in the Ku Klux Klan, race riots, etc. the word redneck has taken on a new connotation: Former President Jimmy Carter's brother Billy describes it this way:

A reckneck is a fella that rides around in a truck, drinks beer and throws the cans out the window.

The most poignant humor is that which parodies life, stretches the truth, exaggerates quirks and character traits. This basic premise is what continues to keep ethnic humor (particularly Polish jokes) America's favorite form of wise-cracking. Some redneck idiosyncracies are also fair game for this kind of funmaking:

Why do rednecks make such good apple pickers?
They've had so much practice with their noses.

Did you hear about the redneck who planted Cheerios in his back yard?
He thought they were donut seeds.

Rednecks come in all sizes, shapes and from all parts of the country. Here is the story of one from the great state of Florida:

Young Ramsey was walking in his yard

when an alligator attacked him. "Mama!" yelled the boy, "an alligator just bit off mah foot!"

"Which one?" called his mother from inside their cabin.

"How the hell should Ah know," shrieked the little redneck, "they all look alike to me!"

Rednecks could be the most misunderstood minority in our nation. Simply because they think our countryside looks better decorated with empty beer cans doesn't mean they aren't nice people. Just because they hate "niggers, kikes, wops, chinks and all furiners" doesn't mean they are *all* bad.

So what if they're frowned upon by Orientals, disliked by Europeans and ridiculed by the majority of decent Americans, rednecks are human beings. What could be more human than two redneck wives sitting in the house sipping a can of beer:

"Oh, shoot," said Mrs. Cantrell. "Look out the window. Here comes mah husband with a dozen carnations."

"Golly," said Mrs. Ledbetter, "wat's wrong with a bunch of carnations?"

"Yew kiddin'? Mah legs'll be spread apart all weekend now."

"Gee whiz, honey," said the other woman, "ain't yew got a vase?"

or:

Did you hear about the redneck housewife who went to the butcher and asked for five karate chops?

So much for redneck power. Bless their cotton pickin' hearts. Rednecks march to a different drummer so we might jes' as well have us a laugh or two. You'll find all them folks right here in this book. Texans and farmers and hillbillies and hootenanny hotshots. Go 'head and open it . . . yawl see what ah mean. . . .

LARRY WILDE

GOOD OLE BOYS

When does a redneck think he's well dressed?

When he has a coated tongue.

*   *   *

Clyde picked up the telephone when it rang. "Hello," said the voice, "this is Wilbur. Come on over, Ah'm having a real wild ass party."

"Shit, Ah'd shore love to," said Clyde, "but Ah got a bad case of gonnorhea."

"Bring it along," said Wilbur, "the way thangs are goin', mah buddies'll drink anythin'!"

*   *   *

Did you hear about the Michigan redneck who had the first penis transplant?

It didn't work out. His hand rejected it.

*   *   *

REDNECK INTELLECTUAL

A man who doesn't move his lips when he
reads.

*   *   *

Kelso and Hensley met on the street.
"Hey," said Kelso, "how come Ah never hear
from yew? Why don't yew call me on the
telephone?"

"But yew ain't got no telephone," said
Kelso.

"Ah know it," said Hensley, "but yew
do!"

*   *   *

Curley and Judd were driving into town for
a big night at the beer joint. "Wot's yore idea
of a perfect gal?" asked Curley.

"Aw," replied Judd, "jes a little ole gal
who screws til two o'clock in the mornin' then
turns into a pizza and a six pack."

*   *   *

Harkins had just joined the police force.
He was assigned duty in a Florida nudist camp.
That night he reported back to the precinct house.

"Well," asked the Sergeant, "how's it
goin'?"

"Real good," said the redneck, " 'cept'n
this here badge is killin' me."

*   *   *

Kennen was having a drink in a saloon. Suddenly, his neighbor Stakely came rushing in and shouted, "Ah think somebody's a stealin' yore pickup!"

Kennen ran out but then returned right away. "Did yew stop him?" asked Stakely.

"Naw, he was too fast," said the redneck, "but Ah got his license plate number."

* * *

Did you hear about the Nebraska redneck who was filling out an application for employment?

In the blank printed "Church Preference" he wrote: *Red Brick*!

* * *

Sheridan and Wyman were passing time down at the general store. "Hey," said Sheridan, "Ah just read that it took that Eyetalian Michaelangelo more'n twenty years to paint the dome of the Sistine Chapel."

"That right?" said Wyman. "Well, the dumb bunny could a done it a lot faster if he got himself a paint roller!"

* * *

Did you hear about the redneck handyman who saw a moosehead on the wall of a room he was painting?

So he said to the boss, "Can Ah go into the next room and see the rest of it?"

A small town in Montana decided to buy a new fire truck. When the village council met they got into a discussion about what to do with the old one:

Randall, an old rancher, stood up. "Ah think," he said, "that we should keep the old fire truck and use it for false alarms."

*   *   *

REDNECK PATRIOT

A good ole boy who will cover an ugly girl's face with a flag and fuck for Old Glory.

*   *   *

What is the most common way for rednecks to commit suicide?
Gluttony.

*   *   *

A complaining Hedges had to have his stomach pumped out and the San Diego doctor wanted to know what he ate to have caused the problem.

"Ah dunno, Doc," said the redneck. "Ah only had a light between-meal snack: six bowls a chili without no ketchup or nothin', a coupla dozen tacos and eight, nine margaritas!"

"I thought so," said the physician, "over indulgence!"

"Naw! Over in Tijuana!"

*   *   *

Despite the scorching July day in Joplin, Oates was painting his house.

A passerby stopped for a moment to watch him and then asked, "How come yer wearin' two jackets?"

"Because," said the redneck, "the directions on the can say'd put on two coats!"

* * *

Did you hear about the redneck who spent two weeks in a revolving door—looking for a doorknob!

* * *

"Hey, Emil, how come yer growin' a beard?"

"Ah got me invited to a Masquerade Bawl," said Clement.

"What the hell yew gonna do with the beard?"

"Ah'm gonna spray mah chin with deodorant and go to the Bawl as an armpit!"

* * *

Jett was trying to light a match. He struck the first match—it didn't work so he threw it away.

He struck a second match. That didn't work either and he tossed it.

Jett struck a third one and it lit up. "That's a good one," said the redneck blowing it out. "Ah gotta save it!"

* * *

"What yew want fer yore birthday, son?" Howe asked his kid.

"Ah want a watch," said the boy.

"Well, if'n it's all right with yore mama, it's okay by me."

If there are three rednecks on a couch, which one is the cocksucker?

The one who's spitting feathers.

*   *   *

Why do haircuts for rednecks cost eight dollars?

The charge is two dollars per corner.

*   *   *

On a Portland construction job Murphy and Lavelli watched in amazement as Simmons kept tapping himself upwards on the elbow.

"What the hell's he doing?" asked Murphy.

"He's goosing himself," replied Lavelli.

"On the elbow?"

"Yeah," grinned the Italian, "you know rednecks don't know their ass from their elbow."

*   *   *

What do you get if you cross a retarded West Virginian with a baboon?

A redneck intellectual.

*   *   *

During a break on a North Dakota office building project a construction worker approached Pyle. "Ah heered the boys is gonna strike."

"What for?" asked Pyle.

"Shorter hours."

"Good for them." said the redneck. "Ah always did think sixty minutes was too long for an hour."

* * *

Why does a redneck eat baked beans on Saturday night?

So he can take a bubble bath on Sunday morning.

* * *

Billy Bob and Bobby Joe were in a bar having a few Falstaffs. Billy Bob was reading the *National Enquirer*. "Says here we only use one third of our brains," he commented.

30 minutes later Billy Joe answered, "Ah wonder what we do with the other third."

* * *

Roach and Tubbs, two Tennessee laborers were working at a State Highway project.

"Hey," shouted Roach, "stop throwin' that dirt out of the ditch!"

"But," said Tubbs, "Ah'm diggin' a ditch and have to throw the dirt somewhere."

"Yew blockhead," said Roach, "jes dig yerself another hole and put it there."

* * *

REDNECK PROPERTY OWNER

A southerner who has made *all* the payments on his false teeth.

* * *

Graves lived in a tiny Alabama town and couldn't get a job. The town council decided to give him the job of keeping the Civil War cannon polished.

The young redneck did a good job and kept the brass polished and the cannon shining.

However, one day Graves went to the mayor's office and informed him he was quitting.

"Why?" asked the mayor.

"Ah been savin' money to buy mah own cannon and go in business for mahself," replied the redneck.

How do you get a one-armed redneck out of a tree?

Wave to him.

*   *   *

Why did the redneck staple his nuts together?

Since he couldn't lick them, he joined them.

*   *   *

Izzard went to an Oklahoma City bank to cash a check. Since Izzard didn't have an account there, the teller asked if he could identify himself.

"Yes'm," said Izzard, "is there a mirror aroun' here?"

"Yes," said the clerk, "on the wall beside you."

Izzard glanced in the mirror and heaved a sigh of relief. "Yeah," he said, "it's me, all right!"

*   *   *

"Do you know how to save a redneck from drowning?"

"No."

"Good."

*   *   *

Did you hear about the redneck who was a bed wetter?

He went to the Klan meetings in rubber sheets.

Moody was awakened by the phone at 4 o'clock in the morning. It was his Ku Klux buddy Gresham calling long distance from Montgomery.

"Whatsa matter?" asked Moody. "Yew in trouble?"

"Naw," said Gresham.

"Whatch yew want?"

"Nothin'!"

"Then how come yer callin' me in the middle of the night?" asked Moody.

" 'Cause," said the other redneck, "the rates is cheaper!"

* * *

FORMAL REDNECK DINNER

When all the men come to the table with their flies zipped up.

* * *

While driving from Chicago to Miami, Coleman stopped at a little roadside diner and began reading the menu.

"What's the difference," he asked the waiter, "between the blue-plate special and the white-plate special?"

"The white-plate special is ten cents extry," explained the waiter.

"Is the food any better?"

"No," said the redneck, "but we wash the dishes."

* * *

Waitress: We got practically everythin' on the menu.

Motorist: So I see. Would you bring me a clean one.

*   *   *

"Ah unnerstand yew come from a tough family, Jenkins."

"You kiddin'? My uncle Russell once slapped Clyde Barrow in the kisser right in front of Bonnie."

"Wow! Ah'd sure like to shake hands with yore uncle!"

"Yew nuts? Yew think we gonna dig him up just for that?"

*   *   *

Marley stopped at the town barber shop for a haircut. After 35 minutes of snipping and cutting, the barber held a mirror in back of Marley's head. "How yew like it?" asked the barber.

"Real fine," said the redneck. "But how 'bout makin' it jes a little longer in the back?"

*   *   *

Did you hear about the survey they took in the Ku Klux Klan?

They found that 1% of them had piles . . . the rest were perfect assholes.

*   *   *

Truitt and Hooks were having a Coors.

"Mah brother ran a hundred yards in six seconds," said Truitt.

"Bullshit!" shouted Hooks. "That's impossible! The world's record is more'n nine seconds."

"Mah brother knows a shortcut."

* * *

REDNECK LOVER

A guy who never leaves a gal in the dark, unless she's coming with him.

* * *

Orville and Dutch, two truckers, were having a smoke while waiting for their names to be called for a load. "Say," asked Orville, "how'd yew make out with that new waitress down at the cafe last night?"

"That gal was one damn pervert."

"Watch yew mean?"

"We was parked down by the creek when she yells, 'gimme 10 inches and make it hurt!'"

"Christ! Wot'd yew do?"

"Ah screwed her twice and punched her in the mouth!"

* * *

What did the redneck say when his sister had a baby?

"Ah'll be a monkey's uncle!"

* * *

For several months Birch had been collecting unemployment checks. When they stopped he decided to become a mailman and went down to take the civil service exam.

The first question was, "How far is the earth from the moon?"

"Look," said the redneck to the examiner, "if'n that's gonna be mah route—yew can forget it!"

*   *   *

Did you hear about the black who told the KKK that he just wanted to be a stud?

So they nailed him to a snow tire.

*   *   *

What do you call 300 Blacks buried up to their foreheads?

Afro turf.

*   *   *

Slaydon was standing in the entrance of a hotel lobby without any clothes on. A policeman grabbed him.

"Okay, Fella," said the cop, "let's get something to cover you and go to the station."

"Wait a minute!" cried Slaydon.

"You can't stand here stark naked!"

"But officer, Ah'm waitin' for mah girl friend," begged the redneck. "We wuz up in the room and she said, 'Let's get undressed and go to town.' Ah guess Ah beat her down."

*   *   *

Grubbs stood in the courtroom. The judge said, "Now, tell me, why did you park your pickup where you did?"

"Whal, yer Honor, there was this sign there that say'd 'Fine for Parking.' "

*   *   *

The teacher asked Jeb the difference between the age of his brother and his own age.

"Mah mother tole me last year," said the redneck, "that mah brother was one year older than me so according to mah calculations, this year we both must be the same age."

*   *   *

Cliff and Jesse were sitting around the general store with a bunch of the boys. "Wanna do some riddles?" asked Cliff.

"Sure," answered Jesse.

"A real dark black man and this real light black guy jumped from the George Washington Bridge at the same exact time. Who hit the Hudson River first?"

"Who cares?"

That got the other rednecks interested. One of them asked, "What do you call a Black with no arms or legs?"

"Trustworthy."

*   *   *

CRYING SHAME

A bus load of rednecks going over a cliff
with two empty seats.

Recently a South Dakota redneck convict filed a brief with the court charging that he was being subjected to cruel and unusual punishment. The Warden had ordered him to take a shower.

* * *

What's the difference between a tire with chains and a Black?
A tire doesn't sing when you put it on.

* * *

How do you babysit a black kid?
Wet his lips and stick him to the ceiling.

* * *

How many Blacks does it take to pave a driveway?
10. If you smooth them out evenly.

* * *

What do you call a Black in a new house?
A burglar.

* * *

What do they call a Black hitchhiker?
Stranded.

* * *

What has six arms and goes, "Ho-dee-doe, ho-dee-doe, ho-dee-doe?"
Three Blacks running for an elevator.

* * *

Why do Blacks wear big wide brim hats?
To prevent birds from shitting on their lips.

*   *   *

Who are the two most famous black women in the world?
Aunt Jemima and Mother Fucker.

*   *   *

Why do Blacks have flat heads?
That's where God put his foot when he pulled the tails out.

*   *   *

How do you stop a Black from jumping up and down on the bed?
Glue Velcro to the ceiling.

How do you get him down?
Bring in some Mexicans and tell them he's a piñata.

*   *   *

Did you hear about the new video game where a large pair of black lips are chasing a watermelon?
It's called Black Man.

*   *   *

What do Thom McAn's and the U.S. Post Office have in common?
They both have 900,000 black loafers.

*   *   *

A freighter sank in the Atlantic Ocean. The only survivors on a small life raft were the captain, a Californian, a Canadian and a redneck.

"Men, there is only room for two of you!" announced the Captain. "I can't play favorites. You are all equal. To decide who must leave the raft I will ask each a question. The man who can't answer the question will have to drown."

"Now," said the Captain to the Californian, "what was the greatest sea disaster?"

"The Titanic!"

"Right! You can stay!" Then to the Canadian: "How many people—approximately—were lost?"

"2,841!"

"Close enough! You too can stay!" Now to the redneck:

"Name them!"

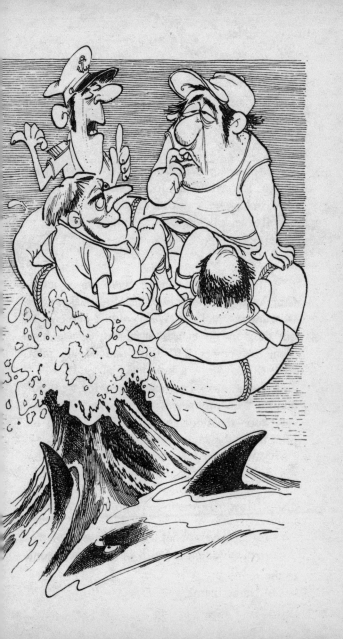

*   *   *

Why do black men always have sex on their minds?

Because they've got pubic hair on their heads.

*   *   *

Mahan stood in front of the take-out window of a Rawlins fast-food restaurant. "I want two hamburgers, one with onions, one without."

Redneck counterman: "Which one?"

*   *   *

Barbour and Linden were on a jet to Cincinnati. Suddenly over the loudspeaker came the captain's voice, "We have lost one engine, but there is no cause for alarm, as we have plenty of power left! But," added the pilot, "the flight will be a little late."

Ten minutes later another engine went out, and the captain repeated the message.

Soon the third engine conked out and the pilot made the same announcement.

"Piss," said Barbour, "if'n that last engine goes out, we could be up here all night."

*   *   *

Did you hear about the redneck who phoned a camera store and asked if he could rent some flash bulbs?

*   *   *

*   *   *

If a Californian, a New Yorker and a redneck went skydiving together and none of their chutes opened, who would be the last one to hit the ground?

The redneck because he would have to stop to get directions.

*   *   *

REDNECK SOPHISTICATE

A guy who doesn't chew tobacco while
he's screwing.

*   *   *

Kelsey was hitchhiking through New Mexico on his way home to Ft. Wayne. He met a Navajo who agreed to tell him the Legend of the Maidens for a dollar.

"According to legend, there are many beautiful Indian maidens who live in large caves and crevices," said the Navajo. "If you hear them call, 'woo, woo', take off clothes quick and enter cave. They will show you good time."

Several days later, the headline in the local newspaper read:

BODY OF NAKED REDNECK
FOUND IN TUNNEL,
RUN OVER BY TRAIN.

*   *   *

Then there was the Kentucky redneck who is asking all his friends to give him their burnt-out light bulbs?

He's starting a dark room.

* * *

How do you get three rednecks off a couch?
Jerk one off and the other two come.

* * *

Did you hear about the Augusta drive-in that showed an old-time melodrama?

During the second reel someone hissed the villain and 38 people got out to look for punctures.

* * *

Down in Florida, a Philadelphian, a Bostonian and a redneck completed the police academy and were close to becoming cops.

"Just one further question," said the police chief to the candidate from Philadelphia. "Who killed Christ?"

"They used to say it was the Jews but they proved that was wrong."

"Good," said the chief. "You start work on Monday."

The former Bostonian entered the chief's office. "Who killed Christ?"

"The Romans."

"Okay. You begin duty Monday morning."

The redneck came in next.

"Who killed Christ?"

"Wal, chief, that's kinda a hard question. Ah'd like to think on it overnight and tell yew tomorrow."

The chief agreed. The redneck went home and his wife said, "Did yew get the job as a cop?"

"Shore did, honey. Ah'm on mah first assignment. It's a murder case."

HITCHIN' AN' HATCHIN'

Who are the six most important people at a redneck wedding?

The preacher, the bride, the groom and their three kids.

*   *   *

Kane paced up and down the Des Moines hospital corridors. Finally, the nurse stopped him.

"Congratulations," she said. "You have twins."

"Real good," said the redneck, "but please don't tell mah wife—Ah wanna surprise her."

*   *   *

Did you hear about the Wyoming redneck's wife who served her husband baked beans with pineapple juice, because she liked Hawaiian music?

*   *   *

Mrs. Swint went to the doctor complaining of being "real tired." After examining her, the physician decided she needed a rest.

"Is it possible for you to stop having relations with your husband for about three weeks?" he asked.

"Shore can," she replied, "Ah got two boyfriends who kin take care of me fer that long!"

*　　*　　*

Did you ever notice that when a redneck family is fighting to keep the wolf from the door, the stork usually comes down the chimney?

*　　*　　*

Vickers was real upset over his 20-year-old son. It seems the boy masturbated several times a day.

"Why don't yew get married?" asked his father.

So the boy found himself a real pretty girl from the same county. A short time later, Vickers discovered his son down in the cellar wacking off.

"Doggone shithead," croaked Vickers. "Ah thought this would all stop, now that yew got hitched to Zelma!"

"But Pappy!" said the boy, "the pore gal— her little arm gets so tired!"

*　　*　　*

In a Nebraska schoolroom the teacher asked young Cletis, "Why don't you smile?"

"I didn't have no breakfast," replied the youngster.

"You poor dear," said the schoolmarm. "Let's get our geography lesson. Cletis, where is the Canadian border?"

"In bed with Mama. That's why I didn't have no breakfast."

* * *

Corporal Calhoun was stationed in Alaska. One day his wife telephoned him from Huntsville.

"We got us a new baby," shouted Mrs. Calhoun. "Born two hours ago."

"Is it a boy or a girl?" asked her husband.

"I dunno," she replied.

"Didn't you look between its legs?"

"Yew nasty man!" said Mrs. Calhoun. "How could yew think about sex at a time like this?"

* * *

In Valdosta Martha Lou and Rebecca Jean were talking about their husbands over the backyard fence.

"If mah husband's big boomerang grew another inch," said Martha Lou, "I couldn't take all of it!"

"Me neither!" said the other redneck wife.

* * *

"How's yore wife, Bubba?"
"Better than nothin'!"

* * *

What is a cad?
A redneck who doesn't tell his wife he's
sterile until after she is pregnant.

* * *

Did you hear about the Oklahoma redneck
who married an American Indian?
They had a baby and wanted a name to
reflect both races. So they named it Running
Dummy!

* * *

Martha Sue and Vorlia May were chatting
over coffee one morning.
"How many kids yew got now?" asked
Martha Sue.
"I got twelve!" answered Vorlia May.
"With so many kids why'nt yew use
sumpin' to stop havin' them?"
"Oh, I use the diaphragm," said Vorlia
May. "Fact is, Ah use it so much Ah keep it
tacked to the headboard of our bed."

* * *

"Our son's teacher says he oughta have an
encyclopedia," said Mrs. Pickens.
"Aw, let him walk to school like I did,"
said Mr. Pickens.

* * *

After the West Virginian wedding, Claude the new bridegroom asked the preacher, "How much do Ah owe yew?"

"Just as much as you think the girl's worth," replied the clergyman.

Claude handed the minister a dollar, which he accepted without comment. Still the couple didn't leave and the preacher thought he might never get rid of them.

"Have I forgotten something?" asked the minister.

"Yes," said the young redneck. "Mah change."

*   *   *

Leon and Floyd were driving home from work. "Let's stop and get a beer at this great new place Ah found," said Leon. "The bar stools are numbered and if yore number is called, yew can go upstairs and get fucked free."

"No shit?" said Floyd. "Did yew ever win?"

"Naw," said Leon, "but last week mah wife won twice!"

*   *   *

At the Louisville Planned Parenthood Center Ginny Sue was asked what she thought of the Loop.

"Ah really couldn't say," she replied, "Ah ain't never been to Chicago!"

*   *   *

Woodard was telling his friend Tippen how he courted and won his wife, even though his father-in-law objected.

"Ah thought it'd be nice to elope," said Woodard. "So Ah put me up a ladder against the side of the house to climb up. When Ah got half way to her room, her father stuck his head out the window and he seed me!"

"What'd yew do then?" asked Tippen.

"Shit, what could Ah do?" said the redneck. "Ah started paintin' the house!"

Sneed was sentenced to jail for having intercourse with his wife's body a few hours after her death.

"Do you have anything to say in your own defense?" asked the judge.

"Honest, yore honor," replied the redneck. "Ah didn't know she was dead. She's been like that fer nigh on to twenty years!"

*   *   *

The Parnells were having their nightly squabble. "Woman," shouted Parnell, "Yore so dumb yew think Barnum and Bailey are married to each other!"

"What difference does it make," said his wife, "as long as they love each other!"

*   *   *

Did you hear about the redneck who won't make love to his wife until she gives him a divorce?

He found out that fucking around with your relatives is incest.

*   *   *

"Ah'm so proud of our little son," said Jawanda. "Do yew know what he was doin' this morning?"

"No, what?" asked her husband.

"He was standin' in front of the mirror with his eyes closed so he could see what he looks like when he was asleep."

*   *   *

"Clovus, how yew manage to get along so good with yore wife?"

"Ah always tell her the truth, even if Ah have to lie a little."

*   *   *

Swayne showed up one morning at work with a big smile on his face. "What yew so happy about?" asked a drinking buddy.

"Monday Ah found mah wife in bed with the electric meter reader!" admitted Swayne.

"Tuesday Ah caught her takin' samples from a salesman on the living room sofa.

"Wednesday mornin', the milkman was puttin' some cream in her on the kitchen table.

"But Ah done fixed them all. No one gets the last laugh on W. W. Swayne. Ah just phoned Goodwill and tole them ta come and pick up our furniture!"

*   *   *

Milford asked for a day off to go to a wedding. His boss agreed. But he didn't come back to work for three days. "Where'n hell yew been?" asked his employer.

"They had a raffle at the weddin' and Ah won second prize!" explained the redneck.

"What'd yew win?"

"Two days with the bride!"

"Well, what was first prize?"

"A turkey!"

*   *   *

43

A redneck who hasn't been born yet.

*   *   *

Arletta had recently married and was proudly telling her mother, Mrs. Sparks, about the bridegroom's new job.

"Guess what, Mama?" said the newlywed. "In my husband's new office, seven girls are under him."

"Yew pore chile," cried Mrs. Sparks, "Ah knew if yew married that sumbitch sumpin' like this would happen."

*   *   *

Bobbi Jean had been married only three days. She walked into a Tulsa drug store and asked for a bottle of men's deodorant.

"The ball type?" asked the clerk.

"No," she replied, "fer under his arms."

*   *   *

What is a redneck no-hitter?

A wedding ceremony before the parson leaves.

*   *   *

Did you hear about the elderly redneck's wife who took birth control pills?

She didn't want to become an unwed grandmother!

*   *   *

Mrs. Clarke, a Mississipian, telephoned the capitol building in Jackson and asked to speak to the Game Warden. After being switched to a number of offices a voice finally said, "Hello?"

"Is this the Game Warden?" asked Mrs. Clarke.

"Yes, it is."

"Oh, thank goodness. At last Ah got the right person. Could yawl gimme some suggestions for a child's birthday party?"

* * *

Izoral said to her husband, "When yew clean yore fingernails this year, could yew do it over the flowerpots?"

* * *

"Say, Arlie, Ah see yer wearin' a new shirt and pants."

"That's right, Otho. Present from the wife."

"No shit."

"Yep. Came home unexpected t'other night and there they was—right on the back of a chair."

* * *

"Eula, marry me," said Buster, "and after our weddin' night yew'll swear I had me a transplant from a mule!"

Eula did, and the next morning she said, "Yew were right about the transplant. Ah wonder what that animal's doin' without his brain."

* * *

Clay took his new teenage wife to the doctor and complained that he could not have intercourse with her because she was too tight.

"Okay," said the doctor, "let's test it!"

The sawbones put Mrs. Clay on the table, applied some Vaseline to his pecker and entered Clay's wife easily.

"Hey," said the redneck, as he watched the doctor pumping away. "If'n it weren't for the medicine I'd think yew was screwin' my wife!"

Norwood's wife died and he moped around the house sobbing and moaning. The next day his brother found him in bed with the neighbor's daughter.

"Whatch yew doin'?" roared his brother. "Yore wife ain't even buried 24 hours and yore screwin' the gal next door!"

"In mah grief," moaned Norwood, "how should Ah know what Ah'm doin'?"

* * *

Naomilee and Betty Jean met on the Memphis Main Street.

"Say," said Naomilee, "Ah heard yew and yore husband is goin' ta night school ta take Spanish lessons. How come?"

"Eh, huh!" answered Betty Jean, "we went and adopted us a little Mexican baby and we wanna be able to unnerstand him when he's old enough ta talk!"

* * *

Lamar's wife gave birth to their first child. Excited with the great news, he rushed to the corner drug store to tell his friends.

"Congratulate me. I'm a father," he shouted to the first man he met.

"Congratulations. What is it—a boy?"

"No—guess again."

"Then it's a girl."

"How the hell did you know?" said the redneck. "Ah ain't tole nobody yet."

* * *

Did you hear about the redneck who thought "no kidding" meant birth control?

* * *

Hicks and Chapman were sitting in the expectant fathers' lounge at the Virginia Baptist Hospital. In a few minutes a nurse walked over to Hicks and said, "Congratulations. You have a little daughter."

Chapman leaped up and shouted, "Hey, that ain't fair. Ah was here first!"

* * *

Peake was working in a meat packing plant. One afternoon he came home and told his wife that he had lost his job.

"How come they fired you?" she asked.

"Fer nothin'!" he said. "They fired me just 'cause Ah put mah finger in the sausage stuffer."

"Well, Ah declare. What harm could yore finger do to a sausage stuffer?"

"That's what Ah can't figure," said the redneck, "but they went and fired her too!"

* * *

Jake and his new bride had just returned from their honeymoon at Myrtle Beach. He began lecturing her about household duties.

"Now, to avoid burnin' your hands in hot water," said the redneck, "feel the water first!"

* * *

Parrish was taking the State Civil Service Exam.

"Have you ever committed sodomy?" asked the psychiatrist.

"No, sir," said the redneck, "one wife is enough fer me!"

*   *   *

The Bradferds were having a big fight. Mrs. Bradferd was terribly upset.

"We're only married five months and already yew got yourself a girlfriend."

"Now, honey," said her husband, "Ah ain't got me no other gal. Yew're the only one!"

"Don't lie to me, yew bastard!" screamed the wife. "This week alone yew washed yore feet three times already!"

*   *   *

Sanger was complaining to his wife that their neighbor kept sneaking up on him and slapping him on the chest and breaking the cigars in his pocket.

"But," said Sanger, "Ah figured out a way to teach him a lesson."

"Watch yew gonna do?" asked Mrs. Sanger.

"Ah'm gonna fix him," said her husband. "The next time he slaps me on the chest, Ah'm gonna have me three sticks a dynamite in mah pocket."

*   *   *

Kinker was bragging to his buddy, "I never have to worry about mah wife cheatin' on me. She's a real, fine, good ole gal—and so goddamned ugly!"

* * *

What is a high class redneck wedding?
When the bride's veil covers most of her overalls.

* * *

In buying gifts for redneck brides, the first question asked is, "What's her jelly glass pattern?"

* * *

Festus said to his wife, "Irlene, now tomorrow why don't you take Junior to the zoo?"
"What do yew mean, *take* him?" responded his wife. "If they want him, they can come and get him."

* * *

The elderly redneck store keeper told his pretty young wife, "Sorry, honey, but Ah'm gonna have to work late tonight."
"Can Ah depend on that?" replied the sexpot.

* * *

Did you hear about the redneck housewife who thinks a can opener is the key to the john?

* * *

That Sunday night after the Knoxville wedding, Fess kissed his teenage bride Eunice on the forehead then rolled over and went to sleep.

For the next six nights he never got any closer to Eunice than an occasional peck on the cheek. Then came Saturday and Fess left right after dinner to join the boys down at the pool hall.

This was the last straw for Eunice and she began to pack her things. Ten minutes later, Fess burst into the room, grabbed his wife, ripped off her clothes, threw her down on the bed and began banging her violently.

"Why . . . a, all of a sudden?" she gasped.

"Well," said the redneck, "the fellers down there at the pool hall tole me yew fuck!"

How do you get a redneck woman pregnant?

Come in her shoes and let the flies do the rest.

*   *   *

Myrtle and Oleta, two Baton Rouge housewives were discussing the problem of getting their husbands up in time for work.

"How do yew get Hubbie out a bed in the mornin'?" asked Myrtle.

"Ah jes open the bedroom door and let the cat in," replied Oleta.

"Does that git him up?"

"Damn right," she said. "He sleeps with the dog."

*   *   *

"It sure took a lot of naggin', but Ah think Ah finally got mah Billy to give up smokin'!" said Mrs. Farrell.

"How'd yew do it?" asked her neighbor.

"He left the house three days ago to get a pack a cigarettes, and he ain't come back with them yet."

*   *   *

"Jethro," said the new redneck bride, "when did yew first realize that yew loved me?"

"When Ah first started gettin' mad at people who tole me you was dirty, dumb, and ugly," answered her husband.

*   *   *

Did you hear about the redneck who divorced his wife because she was giving car salesmen demonstration rides?

* * *

Studdard, an elderly Key West fisherman was sitting with his wife beside their radio.

They had accidentally tuned in to a Southern faith healer. "All yew folks out in radio land, I wanna heal y'awl," the voice boomed. "If yew follow mah directions, yew will be healed. Now, put one hand on the radio and one hand on the part that needs healin'."

Old Studdard put one hand on the radio and the other one on his crotch.

"Whatch yew doin'?" asked his wife. "He said he could heal the sick—not raise the dead!"

TEXAS TWO-STEPPERS

Skidmore pulled his son away from a group he'd been jawing with at a Beaumont barbecue.

"Son," said the Texan to his offspring, "Ah just heard you asking that man what state he was from. Now, my boy, Ah want you always to remember this: if a man comes from Texas he'll tell you; and if he doesn't there's no need to embarrass him."

* * *

A Bostonian at a Miami hotel was boasting to the other guests, "Up in Boston we can start putting up a sixty-story building this month and have it finished by next month."

"That's nothin', son," said a Texan. "Down in Dallas, Ah see them just layin' the foundations when Ah go to work in the mornin', and when Ah come home at night they're already puttin' the tenants out for not payin' the back rent."

* * *

57

TEXAN

The bastard son of a Mexican who ran out
of money on his way to Oklahoma.

* * *

When George Washington was very young
he and his father lived on a big ranch in East
Texas. One day George's dad went out to the
west forty to mend some fence. While he was
gone, George went out to play.

Between the barn and the main house there
was a beautiful cypress tree. George's daddy
loved that tree. Not just because it was a magnificent cypress but because it was the only tree for
fifty miles in any direction. Long after sundown
George's father returned from the range to find
the cypress lying on its side.

"Son," he said, "what happened to my
tree?"

"Ah did it," said George. "Ah cut it down
with my trusty Bowie knife. Ah cannot tell a
lie!"

"Yew'll never get along in Texas, son,"
said his father. "Pack up yore things, we're
moving to Virginia."

* * *

How come you don't see Texans ski much?
If God wanted Texans to ski, he would've
made bullshit white.

* * *

What would you get if you crossed a Texan with a pig?

Nothing. There are some things even pigs won't mess with.

*　　*　　*

Joe Ed and his neighbor Billy Bob were taking an afternoon ride through the foothills.

"Ole buddy," moaned Joe Ed, "Have Ah got me an absent-minded milkman."

"Watch yew mean?" inquired Billy Bob.

"Well, mah wife's been feelin' kind a porely these past couple of days, so Ah stayed home today and took care of her. Early this mornin' there was a knock on the door and Ah went to answer it. Ah was nekkid so Ah threw on mah wife's bathrobe."

"So?"

"When Ah opened the door that danged fool of a milkman grabbed holt a me, started rubbin' mah ass and then gimme a big kiss. Ah reckon his wife must have the same color bathrobe as Ellie Jo's!"

*　　*　　*

TEXAS GENTLEMAN

A fella who'll screw the maid in his wife's bed, when his wife is away on a trip, then makes the maid ride in the backseat when he drives her home.

*　　*　　*

59

For years, La Farge, a Canadian, had heard about everything in Texas being bigger.

So he traveled to the Lone Star State, entered a restaurant and ordered a small steak. When it arrived it was so big that it was served on a huge platter.

"I asked for a small steak," he complained.

"This is small," said the waiter.

Next La Farge asked for a glass of beer and was served a large pitcher. When he finished the beer he asked for the rest room and was told it was the second door on the left.

Being a little drunk, La Farge walked to the second door but turned right and fell into a pool. Instantly he started screaming, "Don't flush it! Please don't flush it!"

A vacationer stopped his convertible by the side of the road near Galveston and watched some workmen digging a huge ditch.

"What's the hole for, fellas?" he asked.

"Wal," drawled one of the Texans, "that's kind of a stoopid question. But if ya'll don't know, ah'll tell yuh. Every once in a while we dig a big hole like this and bury all the SOB's around here in it."

"Isn't that interesting," said the tourist. "And tell me, when you've put all the SOB's around here into that there hole, who's going to be left to cover it up?"

*   *   *

With a posse still hot on his trail
He was tempted by nookie for sale;
   So the Kid went to bed
   With a price on his head
With a girl with a price on her tail.

*   *   *

Rundell was showing some people around his ranch and casually mentioned that he had 3,000 head of cattle.

"But nearly everyone in Texas has 3,000 head of cattle," said one visitor.

"In the freezer?" asked the Texan.

*   *   *

What do they call the vice squad in Houston? Pussy posse.

*   *   *

Pruitt was sitting with some cattle buyers in a Kansas City restaurant swigging a Dr. Pepper. "You got any fast horses on your ranch?" asked one of the men.

"Ah got the fastest horse in the state," said the Texan. "One day, Ah was fifty miles from mah spread when a storm came up. Ah turned the pony's head for home, and he raced the storm so close for the last ten miles that Ah didn't feel a drop. But mah dog, who was only ten yards behind at first, had to swim the whole distance."

*　　*　　*

Ralston came north to Indianapolis to sell a truckload of cows. He picked up a woman in a beer parlor and they went home to her place. They belly-wrestled for a while then the Texan lay back, lit a cigarette, and proceeded to give the bored lady his downhome philosophy.

"Darlin'," crowed the yokel, "Ah been everywhere, done ever' thang, and when mah time comes Ah wanna die with mah boots on."

There was a furious knocking on the door.

"Better put your boots on quick, honey," said the lady. "Because here comes my husband the cop."

*　　*　　*

Why does Dr. Pepper come in a bottle?
Because his wife died.

*　　*　　*

*　　*　　*

A Wichita Falls millionaire called his girlfriend's apartment in Dallas and the maid said her mistress couldn't come to the telephone.

"She's in bed with laryngitis," said the maid.

"God damn those Greeks," barked the Texan and hung up.

*　　*　　*

At a Washington, D.C., costume ball given by Texas society, Valerie arrived wearing the map of Texas as her costume.

Later that night, she was chatting in the library with a fellow she'd just met when, all of a sudden, Valerie slapped him in the face and stormed off.

The guy's friend asked, "What the devil happened?"

"Beats me," he answered. "All Ah know is that when she asked me where Ah was from and Ah put my finger on Amarillo, she let me have it!"

*　　*　　*

In the early days of the Old West many cowpokes thought that sex was a pain in the ass. Of course, that was before Vaseline was discovered.

*　　*　　*

*   *   *

Hatton had raised his two sons alone and decided it was time they learned something about women. "Boys, Ah've taught yew to read and write and to take care of a ranch, but there's somethin' about life yawl have to learn fer yoreself. Now yew both go to a bar in town. Yew'll be approached by girls and yew jes' go with them and they'll show yew what to do."

The two brothers went to the town saloon. After ordering a beer, two girls asked them if they'd like to come up to their room. They agreed. The girls took off their clothes and gave each brother a rubber. "Here, put these on. That way we won't get pregnant." Both boys followed instructions and soon they learned what love making was all about.

A week later while mending the corral fence, one brother said to the other, "Do yew really care whether or not them girls get pregnant?"

"No, Ah don't give a shit!"

"Good, then let's take off these gol-durned rubbers!"

*   *   *

A charmer from old Amarillo,
Sick of finding strange heads on her pillow,
    Decided one day
    That to keep men away
She must stuff up her crevice with Brillo.

*   *   *

"Son, I don't want to see you goin' with that wild girl no more!"

"Aw, shucks, ma, she ain't wild. Anybody can ride her!"

Ranchers Parker, Baston and Loomis went to Africa on a safari. On the return flight their plane crashed and they were brought to a Moroccan hospital. Now, in Morocco, shepherds bring their flocks into town to graze.

One day, after being confined to their hospital room for several months, the Texans looked out their window and saw a herd of sheep enjoying a grass lunch. Parker pointed to a plump ewe and exclaimed, "Ah shore wish that one was Dolly Parton!"

"Ah shore wish that was Bo Derek," said Baston.

"Ah just wish it was dark!" said Loomis.

* * *

TEXAS

A place where men are men and sheep are scared to death.

* * *

Billy Joe Bob was getting the best of his friend, Tipton from New Mexico. "Well," said Tipton finally, "At least we don't need any insane asylums in New Mexico!"

"What do yew do with yore crazy people? Let them run wild?"

"Nope," said Tipton, "we send 'em to Texas and you elect 'em to public office."

* * *

LONE STAR STATE BUSINESS GIRL

One who goes down for dear old Texas.

*   *   *

Treadwell had a small farm with just a few sheep. One day while his wife was dyeing some wool blankets green, a little lamb fell into the bucket of dye. A tourist driving by saw the lamb with the green fleece and bought it for $75. Treadwell figured he had himself a good thing and began coloring more lambs, which soon brought in some big bucks.

"Pretty soon," he bragged, "Ah was colorin' them pink, blue, yellow, green, lavender, and you know—now Ah'm the biggest lamb dyer in Texas."

*   *   *

The University of Texas is considered *the* university in Texas. However, that doesn't stop UT students from telling jokes on each other. Here's some that are sweeping the campus:

What's the difference between a University of Texas coed and a buffalo?
About 25 pounds.

How can you even it up?
Force feed the buffalo, or shave the coed.

*   *   *

What's the difference between a UT coed and a toilet?

A toilet doesn't follow you around for a week after you've used it.

* * *

How do you get a UT coed through a door?

Grease the door frame and dangle a Twinkee on the other side.

* * *

What's the difference between a UT coed and a squad car?

It takes *two* squad cars to block a road.

* * *

What's the difference between garbage and a girl from the University of Texas?

At least garbage gets picked up once a week.

* * *

And how about the UT coed who went to the big homecoming game and came home with a bad case of athlete's fetus?

* * *

What's the difference between Texas fleas and other fleas?

Texas fleas own their own dogs.

* * *

*　　*　　*

At one of the larger Vegas hotels, a man in a Stetson approached a hooker. "What're yore rates?" he asked.

"I'm size-oriented, Tex," she replied. "I charge fifty for average size, sixty for an over-sized whang and seventy-five bucks when a guy is hung maybe nine inches."

"I'm shore sorry, then," sighed the Texan, "but I don't have nothin' smaller'n a hunnerd on me."

*　　*　　*

A woodpecker came to Texas from another state and set to work on a tree. While he was pecking away lightning struck the tree splitting it down the middle. "It beats hell how hard your pecker can get when you're away from home," he said.

*　　*　　*

Old Wyatt confided to his best friend, "Ah'm almost 70 years old. Ah've got almost a million in the bank. Ah've fallen crazy in love with a fiery young redhead. Do yew think Ah'd have a better chance of marryin' her if Ah told her Ah'm only 50?"

"Fact is, Ah think you'd have a better chance if yew told her you're 80!" said his friend.

*　　*　　*

Did you hear about the Texas cowgirl who had the biggest posse in El Paso?

*   *   *

While driving on Highway 87 near San Angelo Miss Desapio had a flat. She got out of her car to open the trunk and get out the spare. As she bent over another car drove up behind. The driver jumped out, pushed down the trunk-lid on the woman, threw up her dress, pulled aside her panty-crotch and screwed her.

The highway patrol found her sitting there weeping, and she reported that she had been raped by a Texan. "Now hold it, lady," said the Texas Ranger, "how'd yew know it was a Texan? Yew said he had yew clamped down in the trunk and yew didn't get free for ten minutes after he was gone."

"That's right," she said, "but he was a Texan all right. I never had anything to do with a man before that had such a great big belt-buckle and such a puny little prick!"

*   *   *

SIGN IN URINALS AROUND AMERICA

Stand Close—The Next Man May Be From Texas

At a fashionable Austin party the caviar ran out. The quick-thinking hostess told the butler to replace it with buckshot and butter. One woman who had eaten the buckshot and commented several times on its excellence, came back after leaving the party.

"Ah simply gotta apologize," she explained. "Just as Ah was walkin' out the door, Ah dropped mah purse. In bendin' down to pick it up, Ah shot yo' canary."

*   *   *

Hoss and Slick were swigging Dr. Peppers and playing dominoes.

"Did yew know that Jesse James was a weight-lifting champion?" asked Hoss.

"Ah don't believe it," replied Slick.

"It's true," said Hoss. "Ah heard he held up two ten-ton trains one after another."

*   *   *

Slim walked into a local post office and noticed a new sign on the wall:

MAN WANTED FOR ROBBERY
IN MONTANA

"Gosh," he said, "if that job was only in Texas Ah'd take it."

*   *   *

73

Nobis went to an Abilene horse sale and began looking at a three-year-old mare. He checked her teeth, examined her eyes, peered into her ears and then shouted to the horse's owner, "Lemme see her twat!"

A hush fell over the crowd. The embarrassed owner stammered, "S'cuse me, but there's women and children here, pardner."

"Ah just wanna see her twat," demanded Nobis.

"Mistah, that's the weirdest request Ah ever did hear of at a horse sale."

"Ah don't know why," offered the cowboy. "If'n Ah can't see her twat, how will Ah know if she can wun in a wace?"

Howard and Melvin, two lions, were walking one behind the other. Suddenly, Howard began to lick Melvin's ass. "Hey," said Melvin, "are you turning into a fairy?"

"No," said the other lion, "I just ate a Texan—I'm trying to get the bad taste out of my mouth!"

*   *   *

Talbert walked into a San Antonio lawyer's office. "Counselor," he said, "Ah wanna divorce."

"Do you have any grounds?" asked the attorney.

"Yeah, Ah got 150 acres."

"No. What I mean is . . . does she beat you up?"

"No. Ah'm up at five o'clock. She's up at eight."

"Look, is she a nagger?"

"No! Damn it! She's a little Mexican broad!"

*   *   *

Why do Mexicans smell?
So blind people can hate them too.

*   *   *

What do they call a sex change in Mexico?
A hole in Juan.

*   *   *

* * *

There are six border towns along the Rio Grande dividing Texas and Mexico. Folks are busy going to the race tracks and bullfights and fiestas and having fun telling jokes. Here's some you'll hear in El Paso nightclubs, Del Rio cafes, Eagle Pass ice houses, Laredo honky tonks, McAllen beer joints and Brownsville bars:

Why do Mexicans have orgasms?
So they'll know when to stop.

* * *

Know the difference between a teacup and a peacup?
A peacup is what a Mexican rides to work in.

* * *

How can you tell a Mexican with a pacemaker?
He's the one with the little jumper cables hanging out of his pocket.

* * *

What do you get if you cross a Polack and a Mexican?
Someone who spray paint graffiti on a chain link fence.

* * *

*　　*　　*

What is the most confusing day in Mexico?
Father's Day.

*　　*　　*

Why do Mexicans have noses?
So they'll have something to pick in the off season.

*　　*　　*

What do you get if you cross a Mexican and a Chinese?
A car thief who can't drive.

*　　*　　*

Why don't Blacks want to marry Mexicans?
They figure the kids'll be too lazy to steal.

*　　*　　*

What do they call a black nuclear physicist in Texas?
Nigger.

*　　*　　*

Historians claim that Sam Houston, in spite of the long hours he devoted to the cause of Texas, still had time to savor the favors of the ladies. He called his favorite girlfriend *Cumberland*. She had the biggest gap east of the Mississippi.

*　　*　　*

*   *   *

Did you hear about the rancher's daughter who was sent home from the county fair 'cause she couldn't keep her calves together?

*   *   *

Suggs strolled into a Philadelphia restaurant wearing high boots and a ten-gallon hat. After ordering he entered the men's room, passed up the urinals and sat down.

A Philadelphian stood there amazed. "I've been curious about you big tough Texans. Why did you squat?"

"Well, suh," replied Suggs. "Ah jes had me a hernia operation t'other day and the doctor tole me not to lift anythin' heavy."

*   *   *

Guidry had on both his six shooters as he entered the drug store. He strolled over to the soda fountain and ordered a hot fudge sundae.

The pretty counter girl smiled at him and asked, "Do you want your nuts crushed?"

"Yew do," said Guidry drawing his guns, "and Ah'll shoot off both yore tits!"

*   *   *

"Say, neighbor, did yew borrow mah hoe?"
"Why, pardner, Ah didn't even know yore wife was in the business."

*   *   *

A fellow whose zipper extends all the way down his left sock.

*　　*　　*

"When I left the ranch I was a three-letter man."

"You mean there were on athletic teams there?"

"No, I sat on a hot branding iron."

*　　*　　*

Shelton ambled into a Nacogdoches saloon and ordered a whiskey. After swallowing the liquid, he turned and noticed another man at the bar. Suddenly, Shelton whipped out his six shooter.

"Get ready to die," said the Texas outlaw. "I'm going to shoot you."

"Why?" asked his victim.

"I've always said I'd shoot anyone who looked like me."

"Do I look like you?"

"Yes."

"Then shoot."

*　　*　　*

Clara Mae staggered into a Ft. Worth bar and asked the bartender for a "Martuni with an olive."

The bartender gave it to her. Ten minutes later she said, "Let me have a martuni with a pickle in it."

The barkeep handed it to her. In a little while Clara Mae said, "Gimme another martuni, but this time leave out the pickle, it gives me heartburn."

"First off, Miss," sneered the bartender, "it's a martini: Second, it ain't supposed to have a pickle in it, and third, the heartburn yew got is because yore right tit is in the ashtray!"

*   *   *

Lureen (to brother):   Jimmy John, your prick is longer than Daddy's.

Jimmy John   :   Yeah, that's what Mama always says.

*   *   *

Levine, a New Yorker in a Honolulu hotel was fascinated by an overweight elderly Dallas couple always snuggling together in the lounge. One day, while the woman went to the Ladies Room he sidled up to the fat old man, "Forgive my being inquisitive," said the New Yorker, "but can you and your wife really get together, as corpulent as you are? You don't have to answer if you don't want to."

"That's okay, sonny," boomed the Texan. "You're the fifth short-peckered New Yorker that's asked me the same question!"

*   *   *

*   *   *

Tatum, who was sitting in a Corpus Christi saloon, tried to butter up the big-busted bartenderess.

"Stay away from me, cowpoke, I'm too hot to handle."

"Wal," said Tatum, "I wasn't fixin' to use my hand, Ma'am. . . ."

*   *   *

In the early days of the Old West a traveling theatrical group was playing to a tough, rough and ready San Antonio audience.

One night as the heroine died, the hero, beside himself with grief, wailed, "What shall I do? What shall I do?"

"Screw her before she gets cold," shouted a voice from the balcony.

That stopped the show cold. Next day the manager went to the sheriff and pleaded, "My company is trying to give the community some high class entertainment—but the audience is spoiling everything by its crude behavior."

"Don't yew worry none," assured the sheriff. "Won't be no more trouble."

That night the sheriff walked in wearing two guns, and sat down in the front row. All went smoothly until a dramatic moment when the hero passionately kissed the heroine and said, "Ah, what could be sweeter than thy lips?"

The sheriff jumped up, waved his guns and shouted, "Ah'll plug the first sumbitch that hollers pussy!"

GOOD OLE GALS

Idonna and Lurleen left Winona to vacation in Santa Monica. One morning they were sunning themselves on a virtually deserted beach.

"This spot is so secluded," said Idonna, "I bet we could go nude into the water."

"What's the use?" asked Lurleen, "ain't nobody 'round to watch us."

*   *   *

"Ain't that Eloise Ann somethin' else?"

"Shore is. She's only 22 and she's already had herself eight husbands."

"Eight?"

"Yep. Three of her own and five of her friends'."

*   *   *

Did you hear about the Ohio redneck's daughter who had two chances to get pregnant? She blew both of them!

*   *   *

While on maneuvers in the Arkansas hills, a squad of soldiers came upon Ada Lynn bent over a washtub scrubbing clothes.

One of the G.I.s crept up behind the girl and had intercourse with her. Ada Lynn went right on washing. Another soldier screwed her, then several more.

After they all left, an old mule rambled over and also boffed her. Without turning around, Ada Lynn said, "Will that last gentleman please leave his name and address!"

* * *

If six girls are wearing raincoats how can you tell which one is a redneck?

She's the one whose slip is showing.

* * *

Lucinda showed up at the Chattanooga bus station with her son.

"Ah wanna ticket and a half for Memphis," announced the young mother.

"Yew can't get by with a half ticket for that boy," said the agent, "he's wearin long pants!"

"Say, if'n that's how yew judge," said the girl, "Ah should ride fer free!"

* * *

After Emmaline heard there was a Peeping Tom in the neighborhood, she cleaned every window in the house.

* * *

Dossie was telling her friend Delta about a strange man who got on at the same station with her. "It was terrible," she huffed. "That asshole grabbed me and kissed me and felt me all up until he had to get off."

"Didn't yew say nothin' to him?" asked Delta.

"Shit no," said the redneck girl. "My momma tole me never talk to strangers!"

*　　*　　*

The following is an excerpt from a recent Rapid City court trial:

"Miss Partlow, you claim this is the man that stole the $100 bill you had pinned inside your brassiere?" questioned the judge.

"Yes, yore honor," she replied. "That's him!"

"Why didn't you put up a fight?" asked the jurist. "How come you didn't scream or kick? You certainly could've scratched him."

"Yore honor, Ah would have," said the girl, "but at that time Ah didn't know he wuz after mah money!"

*　　*　　*

"Hey, L.C., how'd yore sister Redeen get that there black eye?"

"She was a jumpin' rope and forgot to put on her bra!"

*　　*　　*

Emma Lee was wheeling her small child in a stroller through a Pine Bluff supermarket. An elderly woman said to her, "What beautiful red hair that child has! Does his father have red hair too?"

"Ah dunno," said the girl. "He never did take off his hat."

Did you hear about the redneck's wife running after a garbage truck this morning, shouting, "Taxi! Taxi!"?

*   *   *

"Ah think May Belle is a right nice gal."
"Long as she don't open her mouth. That gal couldn't tell which way an elevator was goin' even if they give her two guesses!"

*   *   *

What is a redneck farm girl's favorite perfume?
Evening in Armpit.

*   *   *

Mrs. Limestone took her teenage daughter to the doctor for an examination.
"Has she ever had intercourse?" asked the physician.
"Ah dunno what that means," said the redneck woman. "But give her some anyway—Welfare is paying for it!"

*   *   *

Alma Lee walked into a drug store and requested a package of three rubbers. "How much are they?" she asked.
"Three dollars," replied the clerk, "and 18 cents tax."
"Oh? So that's how they hold those things on!"

*   *   *

Did you hear about the redneck girl who swallowed a pin when she was a child, but didn't feel a prick until she was sixteen?

*   *   *

Loma got her first waitress job in a Little Rock coffee shop.

"It took me all mornin' to fill up this here salt shaker," said the girl to her new employer.

"Why all mornin'?"

"It's real hard gettin' the salt through those little holes on the top."

*   *   *

La Wanda, a pretty blonde got on a crowded Nashville bus and stood near a young fellow.

The fellow thought about giving her his seat so he looked up and said, "How far?"

"Why yew shithead!" snapped the girl. "Would Ah ask yew *how long*?"

*   *   *

NEW ORLEANS NYMPHOMANIAC

A gal who has a good tail and wants to spread it all over town.

*   *   *

"Sam, how does yore daughter like bein' newly hitched to that soldier boy?"

"Real fine. This mornin' she wrote to the army for his favorite food recipes."

*   *   *

*   *   *

Gailard wasn't too experienced at love making. He was in back of his pick-up truck with a real hot tamale but unfortunately wasn't giving her what she wanted.

"Ah'm sorry," he apologized, "Ah'm jes all thumbs tonight!"

"Ah knew yew was usin' the wrong finger!" she snapped.

*   *   *

Rosella, a real pretty North Carolinian, sat in the doctor's office. The M.D. took her name, background and then said, "In order to find out what's wrong with you, I'll have to give you a thorough examination. Please get completely undressed."

"Okay, doc," said the Southern beauty, "but to make me feel right, *yew first*!"

*   *   *

Did you hear about the ambidextrous redneck secretary?

She takes dictation on both her knees.

*   *   *

Corrine Sue was seen with a truck driver in back of the cafe. "No," she cried. "Ah'm not that kind a gal. Besides, the grass is wet, Mama said Ah shouldn't, and two dollars ain't enough!"

*   *   *

A Tucson housewife was interviewing a new redneck maid. After asking her several questions, the woman asked her if she had any religious views.

"No," said the redneck girl, "but Ah got me some good pictures of Disneyland and the Hollywood Wax Museum."

*   *   *

How can you tell Dolly Parton's kids in a crowd?

They're the ones with stretch marks on their lips.

*   *   *

"Mah son is real smart," declared a redneck mother. "He's only six, and he can already spell his name backwards and forward."

"What's his name?"

"Bob."

*   *   *

A Nebraska mother was told that her son was illiterate.

"That ain't so!" she replied angrily. "We wuz married a year before he wuz born!"

*   *   *

Why do redneck mothers have such huge arms?

From raising dumbbells.

*   *   *

Vonda got a job as housekeeper at the Governor's house.

Dusting too hard one morning, she broke the marble penis of an ancient Greek statue. Vonda found some glue and put the marble male organ back in place, but in an erect position.

Later, the Governor's wife spotted the damage. "Vonda," she shouted. "How could you do such a thing?"

"Look, lady," said the redneck maid, "all of them things Ah ever seed looked like that."

Ruby Alice walked up to the desk of a Bowling Green hotel and signed the register with an—"O".

"Why did you put down that circle?" asked the clerk.

"Ah can't write."

"Then why didn't you sign an 'X'?"

"Ah used to sign it that way," said the redneck woman, "but when Ah got me a divorce, Ah took mah maiden name!"

*   *   *

Pregnant Ida Mae stood watching the square dancers from a corner of the hall. She was getting pissed off at everybody inquiring about her health. One of her high school classmates came over and asked, "How yew feelin' these days?"

"Not too good," said the future mother. "Yew know, Ah've missed six or seven periods now and it's beginnin' to worry me."

*   *   *

Riding a train through Oklahoma the woman looked up from her movie magazine and said to her small son, "No, Homer, Ah dunno the name of that there station we just stopped at. Why do yew ask?"

"Because little sister just got off there," replied the boy.

*   *   *

How can you tell when a Georgia cocktail waitress isn't wearing any panties?

By the dandruff on her shoes.

* * *

Mrs. Plyer picked up a phone: "Doctor, come quick. Little Roscoe has swallowed mah fountain pen!"

"I'll be right over," said the doctor. "What're yew doing in the meantime?"

"Ah'm usin' a ballpoint."

* * *

Did you hear about the pregnant Georgia Cracker's daughter who hired a private detective?

She wanted him to find out whether the baby was really hers.

* * *

An Arkansas country gal decided to confess to her boyfriend. "DeWayne, Ah'm afraid Ah should a told yew before this. Ah come from an alcoholic background. Ah was a senior in high school before Ah learned that toast was also a piece of bread."

* * *

There is a way to tell the difference between a high class redneck lady from a poor white trash redneck woman.

The high class redneck lady doesn't dunk her doughnut past the knuckles.

* * *

A wealthy and important Mississippi cotton grower invited Bateman, a New York manufacturer, to be his house guest.

One afternoon the Mississippian walked into the house and found Bateman screwing his daughter on the bathroom floor.

"Ellie Sue!" he shouted at the girl. "Where is yo' Southern Hospitality. Arch yo' back and get the gentleman's balls up off that cold marble floor."

Connie Sue left Alabama and got herself a job in Detroit. She became friendly with a Michigan girl who complained, "Horny men are all alike."

"Horny men are all ah like, too," admitted the Southern gal.

*   *   *

"What'd yew do after work yesterday?" asked Cindy Lou.

"Ah had more fun last night," said Cherl Sue. "Ah went up to my room and hid in back of the door, and when Ah came in Ah said, 'Boo'—and wuz Ah surprised!"

*   *   *

"Mah sister Laverne went and flunked her driver's license test!"

"Ain't that a shame."

"Yeah. When the car stalled, from force of habit, she jumped into the back seat."

*   *   *

Overheard at Grand Forks card shop:

"May I help you, Miss?"

"Ah hope so. Do yew have any Father's Day cards that begin, 'To whom it may concern?' "

*   *   *

What is a redneck clothes dryer?
The back fence.

*   *   *

"Hey, Arlie, how's yore sister Cleola doin'?"

"She wuz doin' fine at her new job at the sanitary napkin factory until the foreman found her puttin' get well cards in each carton."

* * *

Hoyt hung around the Diamond Dance Palace all night buying drinks for Cerise, the bottomless go-go dancer. Later, when they got to her apartment, she pointed to the wall and proudly stated, "Ah had that framed fer good luck. It's the fust dollar bill Ah ever snatched."

* * *

Barbie Ann went to a Wheeling cafe to get a job as a waitress. After the usual questions the owner looked her up and down and then asked, "Yew a virgin?"

Realizing the job might depend on what she said, Barbie Ann replied, "Yeah, but Ah ain't a fanatic about it."

* * *

Irma Jean had a man arrested for rape. They were both in court and the judge asked when the rape took place.

"Yore honor," cried the girl, "Ah don't remember 'xactly, but seems like it was rape, rape, rape, all June, July and August!"

FARMIN' AN' FUSSIN'

The phone in Lackey's Kansas farmhouse rang one evening. When he answered the operator said, "This is long distance from Chicago."

"Ah know it's a long distance from Chicago, so how come yew called me?" asked the farmer.

* * *

Morse bought a rooster from Mrs. Poagie but did not pay her, as she had no change. Later Morse said to her husband, "Say, here's a $10 for that cock Ah got from yore wife."

"It's okay, just keep it," said Mr. Poagie. "Ah never give *your* wife anything."

* * *

Did you hear about the woman who called her husband, "Double Arkansas" because of his two Little Rocks?

* * *

A Georgia farmer's wife shouted, "Zeke, where's yore paw?"

"He's down at the barn juicin' the cows," answered the boy.

"Well, yew take these milk buckets down there and tell him he'd better bring back some *milk*!"

*   *   *

Wilcox was busy working the north forty when his little son Clem came running up. "Papa," he said, "a man just drove up to the house in a great big automobile."

"Clem," said the weary farmer, "run back to the house as fast as you can and ask that man what type of work he does. If he says he's a travelin' minister, run down to the cellar and lock up my liquor cabinet. If he says he is a law officer, lock the garage where Ah keep the still. If he says he's a salesman—sit on your ma's lap and don't move til Ah get there!"

*   *   *

Corabella, a pretty young lass,
Had a truly magnificent ass:
   Not rounded and pink
   As you possibly think—
It was gray, had long ears, and ate grass.

*   *   *

Wanda was born in Philadelphia but fell in love with Elmer, a farmer, at a city block dance. They were married and she moved to her new husband's farm.

The first week there Elmer had to leave.

"Wanda, the artificial breeding man is a comin' out to impregnate one of our cows," said her husband. "Ah gotta go to town, so Ah drove a nail in the two by four over the right cow's stall. Yew show him the cow and he'll take care of it."

The man came and Wanda took him down the row of cows in the barn until she saw the nail. "This is the cow," she said.

"How do you know?" asked the man.

"By the large nail over its stall," she said.

"What's that for?" he asked.

"I guess it's to hang your pants on," said the redneck girl. "Can I watch?"

*   *   *

Some farmers were sitting around the country store when a traveling salesman walked in, pulled up his overcoat, and backed up to the stove.

"Are yew from Iowa?" asked Whittier.

"Yes, I am," said the traveling man, "how did you guess?"

"My wife is from Iowa," replied the farmer, "and she's got the coldest ass of anybody Ah ever saw."

*   *   *

Shelby, a South Carolina farmer kept lifting his pig up to a tree to eat an apple growing there.

A passerby saw him doing this and said, "Why don't you take a bunch of apples and put them in a trough? It'll save you time!"

"Yew asshole," sneered the redneck, "pigs don't care about time!"

A farmer once wrote to Sears Roebuck and Company to ask for the price of toilet paper. He received an answer directing him to look on page 307 of their catalogue. "If I had your catalogue," he wrote back, "would Ah ask you for the price of toilet paper?"

* * *

Did you hear about the redneck farmer's daughter who suffered a fate worse than death to pay off the villain who held a mortgage on the family farm—and enjoyed it so much she went out looking for the guy who held the second mortgage?

* * *

The farmer called his daughter to supper. "I'm comin'!" she answered from behind the barn, "in just two seconds!"

Then she whispered, "Hurry, honey! Ah never lied to my Daddy in my life!"

* * *

"Where you goin', Calvin?"
"Town."
"What's the matter with that wheelbarrow?"
"Broke."
"Who broke it?"
"Hired man."
"Same hired man who got your daughter in trouble last year?"
"Yep. Clumsy, ain't he?"

* * *

Did you hear about the redneck farmer who gave his wife a washing machine for her birthday but had to get rid of it?

Every time she got into it, she came out black and blue!

*   *   *

Wesley went to a farm house and knocked on the door. "Ah wuz at the wheel of that pick-up truck down the road when the load of horse manure overturned a while ago . . ."

"C'mon in," said Farmer Thompkins. "Yew come to the right place fer help. But furst have a cold glass a cider."

"No," said Wesley, "Paw wouldn't like it."

"Aw. Have yoreself some cider!" insisted the farmer.

"Paw wouldn't like it," said the boy but he nevertheless drank the cider.

"Now, how about some supper?" said Thompkins.

"No," said Wesley, "Paw wouldn't like that either."

"Listen, son," said the farmer again, "Yew gotta have sumpthin' to eat." And the boy did.

When they had finished the farmer pushed his plate back and said: "We'll go down now and reload the horse manure. By the way, where's yore Paw?"

"Under the horse manure," said the youngster.

*   *   *

Gloria, a Pittsburgh secretary, was driving on the back roads of Pennsylvania when she noticed Vernal, a plow boy, stop his farm work to pee against a rock.

Fascinated by the size of his pecker the girl seduced him. But Vernal was young and didn't know what to do.

"Put it in," she purred in his ear, "and now pull it out. And now push it in."

"Say," said the redneck, "Ah wish yew'd make up yore mind. Ah still got six acres of land to plow!"

* * *

Tolbert and Leddy met on the main street of a small Indiana town. "Hey," shouted Tolbert to the other farmer. "If'n yew kin tell me how many chickens Ah got in this bag, Ah'll give yew both of 'em."

"Three!" guessed Leddy.

"T'ain't fair. Yew looked in the bag!"

* * *

Did you hear about the redneck farmer who ran a steam roller across his fields because he wanted to market mashed potatoes?

* * *

Folsom had a prize Virginia bull. One morning he discovered that the animal had crossed eyes, so he went to Lynchburg for the veterinarian. The vet stuck a stiff plastic tube in the bull's rear, blew hard and the bull's eyes uncrossed.

But a week later, just before Folsom planned to show the bull at the County Fair, the animal's eyes crossed again.

The farmer got Delmore, his hired hand, and said, "Yew watch the bull's eyes!" Folsom then put the stiff tube in and blew and blew. Nothing happened.

"Delmore," said the farmer, now out of wind, "Yew blow awhile and Ah'll watch his eyes!"

Delmore began removing the tube and Folsom boomed, "What in the hell are yew pullin' the tube out for?"

"Well," replied the redneck, "yew don't think Ah'm gonna blow on same end as yew, do yew?"

*   *   *

Shelton caught the hired man and his wife in bed. The hired man jumped up, buttoning his fly, grabbed his hat, and began edging toward the open door.

"Guess I can't stay on now!" he said. "I'll pack up and go!"

"Now don't get discouraged," said the old farmer. "If the two of us can't keep the old woman satisfied, why, we'll just have to hire another man!"

*   *   *

Wade was in the big city getting his first professional haircut. After seeing the manicurist with a 40-inch bust in an extremely low-cut white uniform, he decided on a manicure too.

The girl bent over Wade's hand for ten minutes working on his fingernails as he stared down at her enormous breasts.

"Now," she said, "would you like your cuticles pushed down?"

"No, ma'am," Wade replied. "If'n the barber'll let me walk around a while with the sheet over mah front, Ah'll be all right."

*　　*　　*

Lockwood walked up to a policeman near the State Fair Grounds in Iowa. "Did yew see a wagonload of hogs go by?"

"Nope. Did you fall off?"

*　　*　　*

Young Jubal took Sherri Lou out behind the barn. "Wanna see how brave I am?" boasted Jubal as he wriggled out of his clothes and sat down on a tree stump. "Look, Ah'm holdin' a snake in mah lap!"

"That sure ain't much of a snake," said the farmer's daughter. "It's head is way too close to its rattles."

*　　*　　*

The census taker asked the little farm boy how many people there were in the family. "There's four," he replied, "Mah Pappy, mah Mama, mah sister, and me."

Then the census taker asked, "Where are they?"

"Pappy's gone fishin', I guess; anyhow his boots are gone, and it ain't raining. Ma's out taking a shit, I guess; anyhow the Monkey-Ward catalogue's missin', and she can't read. My sister's out in the barn screwin' the hired man, ah guess. Anyhow, there's only two things she likes to do, and supper's been waitin' on the table now, nigh onto two hours."

*　　*　　*

Rowlett was being examined by a doctor. "Why do you have the word *International* tattooed in reverse on your back?" asked the physician.

"That's not a tattoo. That's where mah pappy's tractor got me when Ah was closing the barn door."

* * *

Reb the farm hand and his girl were out riding in a buggy one night. Suddenly, the horse raised its tail and began releasing an endless shower of water.

The girl, pretending not to notice, looked up at the sky and said, "Where is the big dipper?"

"Aw," said the redneck, "Yew don't need it—that stuff ain't fit ta drink!"

* * *

Holton discovered a traveling salesman making love to his wife out in the barn and knocked him out cold. When he came to, the salesman found his penis clamped in a bench-vise and the handle of the vice broken off. Holton was sharpening a butcher-knife.

"My God!" cried the salesman, "you're not going to cut it off!"

"No," said the farmer, "yew can do that. Ah'm gonna set the barn on fire!"

* * *

Zeb asked the school librarian for a good book to read.

"Do you want something light?" asked the librarian. "Or do you prefer a heavier book?"

"It really don't matter none," said the boy, "Ah got mah truck outside."

*   *   *

Lewis decided to quit toiling as a farm hand and get work in a grain factory. He filled out a job application and later was being interviewed by Newley, the personnel manager.

Newley noted that Lewis didn't fill in the year of his birth. "I see that yore birthday is November 6," said the personnel manager. "May Ah ask what year?"

"Every year!" said the redneck.

*   *   *

The public opinion poll taker was speaking to a typical Iowa farmer.

"Now tell me the truth," said the pollster, "would you rather see your daughter married to a redneck or to a circus monkey?"

"It depends," said the farmer. "Does the monkey work steady?"

*   *   *

*　　*　　*

"Idella promise you'll always remember me!"

"Of course, Waldo. How could Ah ever forget yore corn liquor breath!"

*　　*　　*

Jetton had borrowed a bull from a neighbor to service his two cows. He put the beast in the pasture and told his son to keep an eye on them. "Soon as the bull's finished, yew come on up to the house and tell me," he said.

When Jetton got back to the house, he found the preacher there paying a social call. They were seated in the front room sipping lemonade when the boy burst in the door.

"Dad, dad," he exclaimed, "the bull just fucked the brown cow!"

Greatly embarrassed, Jetton took his son outside. "That ain't no way to talk in front of the reverend," he scolded. "Yew could've said the bull 'surprised' the brown cow. Go back down to the pasture and come tell me when the bull is finished."

Ten minutes later the boy dashed into the room again.

"Dad! Dad!" he exclaimed.

"Ah know," said the farmer, "The bull has surprised the white cow."

"He sure has," exclaimed the boy. "He screwed the brown cow again."

*　　*　　*

Slover gathered his five sons around him and demanded, "Which one of yew boys pushed the outhouse into the creek?"

Calvin, the guilty one, remained silent. "Now, boys," said the farmer, "remember the story of George Washington and the cherry tree. Young George chopped down that tree, but he tole his father the truth, and his father was proud of him."

Calvin then stepped forward and admitted that he had pushed the outhouse into the creek. The farmer picked up a strap and whipped the boy for a solid ten minutes.

"But, Pa," protested the youth, "yew said George Washington's father wuz proud a him when he confessed to choppin' down the cherry tree."

"He wuz. But George Washington's pappy wasn't sittin' in the damn cherry tree when his son chopped it down."

Quitman drove into Phoenix with his girl to catch their first play in a theater. Quitman rushed up to the box office and said, "Gimme two tickets for tonight's show."

"Sorry, there are no seats left," said the box office man. "We have only two standing rooms left."

"I'll be hog-tied. Only two left in standing room?" asked the redneck. "Are they together?"

*　　*　　*

Why do farmers have brown toes?

From kicking people in the ass for telling farmer jokes.

*　　*　　*

Alonzo visited Chicago for the first time. He was trying to cross State Street one evening. The light was red so he waited. Then a green sign lit up. It read: WALK. So the redneck got out of his truck and crossed the street.

*　　*　　*

Horace walked into a Macon carpentry shop. "Lissen," he said, "can yawl make me a box 36 feet long and 1 inch square?"

"Never built nothin' like that before," replied the carpenter, "but Ah could do it. Why yawl want a box 36 feet long and 1 inch square?"

"Mah neighbor Perkins moved to North Dakota," said the redneck, "and left his garden hose and now he wants me to ship it to him."

*　　*　　*

* * *

Did you hear about the farmer in Wisconsin, who had a son who went to New York City and became a bootblack?

Now the farmer makes hay while the son shines.

* * *

Barton, a tractor salesman, got caught in a severe Minnesota blizzard. Unable to drive, he trudged to a nearby farm house. The farmer said, "We're short of beds, but you can sleep with my daughter."

So they went to bed. Minnie was 18 and had a brassiere model's figure, and soon Barton made a pass at her.

"Stop that!" she said. "I'll call my father." He stopped. But 20 minutes later he tried again.

"Oh, stop . . . that," she said. "I'll call my father." But she moved closer to him; so he made a third try. This time no protest. Just as Barton was about to drowse off, she pulled at his pajama sleeve.

"Could we do that again?" she murmured. They did and this time he fell asleep, only to be awakened by the tug at his sleeve.

"Again?" And again he obliged.

In a few minutes the girl woke him again by tugging on his pajamas. Barton mumbled, "Stop that or I'll call your father!"

* * *

Did you hear about the redneck farmer who was so stupid his wife had to stamp on her stomach, *This Side Up?*

* * *

Stacey decided to take his wife and 17 children to the County Fair.

Once there, they all wanted to see the exhibit with the prize bull. But tickets were $5 each and the poor man was frantic at the thought of spending all that money.

He approached the ticket seller and said, "Mister, Ah got me a wife and 17 children. Couldn't you let us go in at half price?"

"17 children?" gasped the amazed official. "Just wait here a minute and Ah'll bring the bull out to see you."

* * *

Zeke and his wife, Emma, got into bed. In a few minutes he reached over and fondled her breasts. "If'n they could only give milk," he said, "we could do away with the cow."

Ten minutes later, he grabbed her bottom and said, "If'n this could only lay eggs, we could do away with chickens."

Suddenly, Emma turned over and took hold of Zeke's organ. "If this could only stand up," she said, "we could do away with yore brother!"

* * *

Thompson and Zunker had been good friends for years. Thompson's oldest boy had been dating Zunker's daughter. One morning the two farmers met and Zunker was really mad. "Say," he boomed, "from now on Ah don't want that boy of yours to set foot on my place."

"Why, what's he done?" asked Thompson.

"He pissed in the snow, that's what he done, right in front of mah house!"

"But there ain't no big harm in that," said Thompson.

"No harm!" hollered Zunker. "Hell's fire, he pissed so it spelled Cora's name, right there in the snow!"

"The boy shouldn't a done that," agreed Thompson. "But Ah don't see nothin' so terrible bad about it."

"Well, Ah do!" yelled Zunker. "There wuz two sets a tracks! And besides, don't yew think Ah know my own daughter's handwriting?"

Little Mordecai ran home shouting, "Gramps, Gramps, guess what I saw!"

"What'd yew see?" asked his grandfather.

"The ole bull tried to jump clear over the cow. And he would have too, only a big red thing came out of his belly and caught her in the asshole!"

*   *   *

"That cow at the fair is worth a million dollars."

"Why's that?" asked Fenton.

"Because it has a cunt like a woman's."

"Well, Ah never!" said the farmer. "And here Ah've got a woman with a cunt like a cow, and it ain't worth a nickel!"

*   *   *

Young Neely was driving through the Michigan backroads when his car broke down. He stopped at old Russell's farm house and asked to stay the night. It was just the elderly farmer and his wife, so they only had one bed. The old man slept in the middle, with his wife on one side and Neely on the other.

About midnight the woman said, "Come on over," but Neely was afraid Russell might wake up. "My husband's a real sound sleeper," said the woman. "If'n you don't believe me, just pull a hair outa his ass."

The young fellow pulled out a hair just like she said, but the old man went right on a-snoring. So he went over and gave the woman what she wanted.

After a while Mrs. Russell said, "Come on over," again. The young fellow wasn't so anxious this time, but she finally got him in the mood. Neely pulled another hair out of the old man's ass, and Russell kept right on snoring. So he crawled over again, and gave the woman all she could handle.

The third time the woman says, "Come on over," Neely didn't want to go. "We'd better let well enough alone."

But the woman kept on fooling around till she got him worked up again. So finally the young fellow jerked out another hair, and this time the old man woke up. "Stranger," said the farmer, "Ah don't mind people screwing mah wife. But yew'll have to quit usin' mah ass for a tally-board!"

*   *   *

Smalley put his pig in a wheelbarrow every morning so that he could take it to a neighbor's farm to mate. He did this for several weeks but nothing happened. One morning the farmer's wife went to the pig pen to see if the pig had shown any symptoms of pregnancy. When she returned Smalley asked, "Well, is she?"

"No, but the pig is waitin' in the wheelbarrow!"

*   *   *

Fernell's outhouse had a two-seater. He was joined there one morning by a redneck cousin visiting from Kansas. When the relative finished and zipped up his pants he shouted, "Damn it!"

"What's the matter?" asked the farmer.

"Ah just dropped 35 cents down the hole!"

"Don't fret about . . . wait a minute, why'd you just throw a 20 dollar bill down the hole!"

"Yew don't think Ah'm goin' down there fer a lousy 35 cents do yew?" asked the redneck.

HILLBILLIES AND HOOKERS

When is a hillbilly wedding considered to be real classy?

When the girl's father brings *two* shotguns.

*   *   *

Cole came down from the hills to buy some grits and tobacco. "How's yer family?" asked the storekeeper.

"Can't say my 12-year-old bride ain't been a comfort to me," replied the hillbilly, "but I can't stand the noise when her and my 13-year-old daughter by mah first wife gits to fightin' over who's gonna play with the doll!"

*   *   *

The Ozark boy of 14 asked his father for a chaw of tobacco.

"You're too young for that, son. Whaddya want it for?"

"Want to get the taste of milk out of my mouth, paw. Maw's been eatin' wild onions again!"

*   *   *

Did you hear about the hillbilly who married a dog?

He had to, it was a shotgun wedding.

*   *   *

"Rollie," yelled the hillbilly mother, "what yew doin' out there in the wood shed so long?"

"Aw, nothin' maw," he shouted back. "Ah'm jes fiddlin' with mah axe handle."

"Well, yew be sure an wash yer hands real good before yew come in to supper."

*   *   *

Riggs opened a checking account and filled out his application by putting two XX's on the signature line. Thayer, the banker, did not seem surprised, and things went smoothly for almost a year. Then one day a check came in with three XXX's instead of the normal XX's on the signature.

Thayer phoned Riggs. "One of yore checks came in today, but it was signed with three XXX's. I thought somebody might be tryin' to forge yore signature and just marked on the extra X by mistake.''

"Naw, it's mine," said the redneck. "Mah girlfriend thought it'd look better if'n Ah started usin' mah middle name.''

*   *   *

NEWS ITEM

A Tornado ripped through West Virginia and caused $6,000,000 in improvements.

*   *   *

From the Kentucky moonshine country comes proof that there is redneck power. Yesterday, two revenuers were found with their heads tied together—shot through the hands.

*   *   *

Jeffcoe brought a younger man who was suffering from a bad leg wound into a doctor's office. "Better look after mah son-in-law here," he said.

"My goodness," said the doctor, looking at the wound. "How did this happen?"

"Ah done shot him!" said the hillbilly.

"You shot your own son-in-law?"

"Wall, you see, he warn't my son-in-law when Ah shot him.''

*   *   *

What do they call it when a redneck Ph.D. marries a Polish dishwasher?

Upward mobility.

*   *   *

A sociologist was speaking to a Tennessee father, "If your daughter came home and admitted she was pregnant by an Alabama redneck, would you rush to get your shotgun?"

"Yew betcha Ah would," said the hillbilly. "Then Ah'd use it to kill myself."

*   *   *

Coy came into town and didn't know that the house of ill-repute had been closed down and in its place was now an office selling used sewing machines. "What kind would you like?" asked the salesgirl.

"Well, how much are they?" asked the hillbilly.

"Some are $50 and some are $100."

"The one I got last time wuz twenty bucks!"

"Oh," said the girl, "that must be the kind you screw on the table."

"No, Ma'am, Ah screwed this one in bed!"

"Oh, those," said the girl, "they're the ones that don't have any legs. You have to screw them on the table."

"Shucks," said the boy. "Ah don't much mind the table part, but durned if Ah can stomach screwing one without legs!"

*   *   *

* * *

Leoma had finished with the john. After paying her he said, "You ever been picked up by the fuzz?"

"Shore I have," said the redneck hooker, "and it hurts like hell!"

* * *

Did you hear about the hillbilly who fit a silencer to his shotgun because he wanted his daughter to have a quiet wedding?

* * *

SCENE IN A MISSOURI SCHOOLHOUSE

Teacher: Wiley, spell mouse.
Wiley: M-o-u-s.
Teacher: But what's at the end of it?
Wiley: A tail.

* * *

Luster, aged 10, walked into the house and said to his mother, "Those new neighbors that just moved in next door shore must be rich!"

"How come?" asked his mother.

" 'Cause down at the general store their little boy bought twice as much cockroach powder as I did!"

* * *

133

Parker had never seen a motorcycle before. While out walking with his daughter one day a motorcycle came roaring down the road. "Shoot, Pa, shoot!" exclaimed his daughter. The hillbilly picked up his rifle and shot five times.

"Did you kill it, Pa?" asked the girl.

"Naw," said Parker. "It's still growlin'. But Ah made it let go of the man it was carryin'."

*   *   *

How did Mobley get to be the fastest runner in the Ozarks?

His trainer told him that if he ever lost a race he'd have to take a bath.

*   *   *

Mayne and Barker, were in a rowboat out on a lake fishing. Suddenly, the spray from a motorboat racing by flooded their boat.

"How we gonna get the water out?" asked Mayne.

"Easy," replied Barker, "We bore us a hole in the bottom of the boat and let the water drain out by itself!"

They drilled a hole in the bottom and more water rushed in.

"Wait a minute!" exclaimed Mayne. "We need another hole so that the water comin' in through the first hole has a place to flow back into the lake!"

*   *   *

Jondi and Wilma, two prostitutes, were chatting at a Murfreesboro bar. "Ain't it a shame about Opal losin' her mind?" asked Jondi.

"No wonder," said Wilma, "she worked in the same cat house with us for ten years, and then she found out we wuz gettin' paid!"

*   *   *

Did you hear about the hillbilly hooker who was so ugly she ended up working in a doghouse?

*   *   *

Mrs. Flack stopped Guthrie on the main street and said, "Shame on you, Ah saw yew comin' out of that whorehouse last night."

"Be quiet, woman! Ah had to come out some time, didn't I?"

*   *   *

Luddy, the moonshiner, hailed an Independence taxi and noticed the driver was a pretty blonde. He decided to have some fun and said, "Take me to the cheapest cat house in town."

"Mistah," retorted the female cabbie, "You're in it!"

*   *   *

Mrs. Dester took her future son-in-law aside before the wedding. "Ah'm kinda worried," said the woman. "Are the men in your family 'built large,' because on the bride's side the women're all 'built small.' "

"Well," asked the groom, "is hers as big as a duck's ass?"

"Of course," said the mother.

"Then, don't worry," replied the groom, "mine is no thicker than a good big duck's egg."

*   *   *

137

Miss Sheffield, a social worker in the Ozarks, saw a woman feeding her baby sops of bread and pan drippings. "That child should be nourished at the mother's breast, if there is no other milk available," said the girl.

"Well, ma'am," said the hill woman, "Ah guess you know, seein' as how you're book learn'd. But you see my oldest boy there? He's purty healthy lookin' ain't he? Well, he never had a tit in his mouth till the night he got engaged!"

*   *   *

Why haven't hillbilly sportsmen entered the Kentucky Derby?

They can't get their racing donkeys to run fast enough.

*   *   *

Mama, watching daughter dress for a party said, "Ain't yew gonna put on no panties tonight, dear?"

"Naw, Ma, hit ain't cold," said the daughter.

"Whyncha go ask grandma what she thinks."

"Grandmaw, if'n yew goes out to have a date with your sweetheart and yew might have a chance to get kissed—yew wouldn't wear no veil, would yew?"

"Naw," replied grandma, "Ah sho' wouldn't."

*   *   *

What is a hillbilly vacation?
Sitting on somebody else's front porch.

* * *

Did you hear about the hillbilly couple who had a double ring ceremony?
They were married in a bathtub.

* * *

"This feudin' 'twixed them Martins and McCoys has got to stop," said Aunt Bertha. "While Jeb and Betsey was parkin' down there in the woods last night a stray bullet from ol' Tater McCoy's squirrel rifle hit poor Betsey in her private place."

"Land o' goshen!" said cousin Ruth. "Did Jeb get hurt?"

"Shore did! It clipped off two of his fingers!"

* * *

Two Clarksville secretaries were chatting over lunch. "I was out with a hillbilly last night and boy was he a numbskull."

"How's that?"

"I invited him to go to bed with me and he said, 'No thanks, I'm not tired . . .' "

* * *

What is Hillbilly matched crystal?
Three empty jars of the same brand of jelly.

* * *

While driving through the Ozarks, Harper spotted a burly mountaineer wrestling with a big bear—and getting the worst of it.

On top of a boulder nearby was the mountaineer's wife, a rifle slung under her arm, watching the entire scene.

"Quick!" shouted Harper, "shoot the beast!"

"Not yet," said the wife, "Ah'm awaitin' to see whether the bear won't save me the trouble."

*   *   *

Otho had been sparking Gaylen's daughter. In order to play up to her father, the boy acted rough and crude.

"Now you're the kind of fella Ah want mah daughter to marry," said the hillbilly, "spit halfway across the room, and snot yourself on the floor—not like them city slickers that blow their nose in a little rubber bag and throw it behind the sofa!"

*   *   *

Did you hear about the hillbilly hooker who was so dumb she wound up working in a warehouse?

*   *   *

The judge stared at the pretty teenage mountain girl. "You're charged with assault and battery on your husband. How do you plead?"

"Innocent," snapped the girl. "Ah hit him 'cause he called me a bad name. He said I wuz just a two bit whore."

"That is bad. What'd you hit him with?" asked the judge.

"A bag full of quarters."

*   *   *

Newton and his friend Elbert were strolling along a Richmond road. After a long silence Newton said, "What seems ta be botherin' yew?"

"Somthin's been eatin' at me fer days,"

said Elbert. "Maybe tain't none of mah business, but yew and me is been friends since kids and Ah just gotta tell ya."

"Go 'head," said Newton.

"Last Saturday night Ah was in a whore-house and who do Ah see there but yore wife, Ada Mae. Ah hate to say it Newt, but Ada Mae's a prostitute!"

"Naw! Ada Mae ain't no prostitute," said Newton. "She's just a substitute. She's only there on weekends!"

* * *

Stover made a lot of money from moon-shining. He decided to have his entire house redecorated. Mrs. Stover insisted on helping.

When the stained glass windows were delivered, she said to the contractor, "Yew take these right out and have all the stains removed!"

* * *

A lanky mountaineer and his young wife came into town on their regular Saturday visit. He held a week old baby in his left arm.

The owner of the General Store hadn't seen the couple in some time. "Howdy folks, good to see yew agin," he said. "Say, now, is that yore young 'un, Festus?"

"Yeah, I recken it's mine," answered the mountaineer. "Leastways, it wuz caught in mah trap!"

* * *

*　*　*

He: Guess I'll go out and paint the town red.
She: You ain't got the brush for it, Pa.

*　*　*

Grandpaw and Grandmaw were sitting out on their front porch in their rocking chairs. Suddenly Grandmaw slapped Grandpaw right out of his chair. "What in tarnayshun did yew do that fer, Maw?" snorted the old man.

"Well, Paw," she said, "that's fer havin' such a little bitty prick all these years."

Grandpaw began to rock again and in a few minutes he suddenly knocked Grandmaw clean off the front porch. The old lady climbed back on the porch, sat down and said, "Now what'd yew do that fer, Paw?"

"Fer knowing the difference, Maw!"

*　*　*

The old couple were looking through the mail order catalogue and came to the tombstone section.

"Maw, when yew die," said the husband, "Ah'm gonna git this tombstone and put on it:
HERE LIES MA, COLD AS EVER."

"Yeah, Paw, but yew'll die fust, and when yew do," said the wife, "Ah'm gonna put on yore tombstone:
HERE LIES PA, STIFF AT LAST."

*　*　*

Ike went to a Louisville theatre and saw his first foreign movie. He watched as the slick French lover began kissing the maid on the ear, the neck, the shoulders, the arm, the fingers and points South.

Ike couldn't stand it and walked out of the movie. "Anything wrong?" asked the manager.

"That stupid foreigner," said the hillbilly. "Don't even know where to kiss a girl."

*   *   *

What is smarter than a smart redneck?
A dumb hillbilly.

*   *   *

Hattie and Lon had just been married, and, since no formal honeymoon was planned, they moved directly into his cabin right after the ceremony.

That night, Luke, a friend who had been unable to attend the wedding, went to the cabin to offer his congratulations. He knocked on the door and the bride opened it all dressed up in her new 'store-bought' clothes. Hattie accepted his congratulations and then remarked that she and Lon were about to go to bed.

"But you're dressed," gasped Luke. "Yew folks goin' to bed with all yore clothes on?"

"Wal," smiled the mountain gal, "Lon said we'd be agoin' to town 'bout eleven o'clock tonight, so Ah can't see the need fer undressin'!"

*   *   *

They had been married only two days. The bride walked out on to the porch where her husband was sitting on a rocking chair.

"Jiminy, Seth," she screamed. "Yer beard is caught fire."

"Ah know it, Ah know it," he answered. "cain't yew see me prayin' fer rain?"

*   *   *

Did you hear about the hillbilly girl who claimed to be a calendar model, but she had a face that would stop a clock?

*   *   *

Larimore walked through the Men's Department of a J. C. Penney in Nashville. He noticed the sales clerk wrapping a pair of pajamas.

"What's that?" he asked.

"Pajamas," replied the clerk.

"What're they fer?"

"You wear them at night," explained the clerk. "Would you like to buy a pair?"

"Nope," answered the hillbilly. "Don't go no place at night 'cept to bed."

*   *   *

Young Hicks went to a whorehouse for the first time. The madame, sensing that he had a lot to learn about sex, fixed him up with Jolene, her most experienced girl. Jolene asked the boy if he was familiar with 69 and when he said "no," she showed him how to do it.

As they were going at it she farted. A little later the girl farted again.

"My God," protested the hillbilly. "Ah can't stand this. Tell me—do Ah have to go through this 67 more times?"

*   *   *

148

"Ah shore wish Ah had mah wife back," sighed old Newt.

"Where is she?" asked a friend.

"Sold her fer a jug of mountain dew."

"Ah reckon yew're beginnin' to miss her."

"Nope. Ah'm thirsty agin."

* * *

Billy had been doing it with girls since he was 12 and he knew all the sexual variations.

One night he was banging a pretty gal from the next county. Just as she was coming for the first time she let out a loud fart.

"Oh, honey, Ah'm so embarrassed," she said.

"That's okay," said Billy. "Yore asshole is just jealous—an Ah'll get to him in a minute."

* * *

The Memphis bus was crowded, and Waylen was crushed into a seat with a pretty girl whose short skirt kept creeping up her thighs. She fought a constant, though losing, battle because she no sooner would pull it down, than it would slide up again.

She finally gave it one hard yank and then looked up to meet Waylen's eyes.

"Don't rip your calico, sister," said the hillbilly. "My weakness is liquor."

* * *

The insurance salesman was trying to sell a policy to the Cranbys. He asked the husband, "How would your wife carry on if you should drop dead?"

"Don't ask me," answered the hillbilly. "Ah can't hardly keep her out of the neighbors' beds while Ah'm alive."

CORNPONE AND
COUNTRY FOLK

Melburn was strolling along downtown
Natchez with a framed picture under his arm.

"Hey, what yew got there?" asked a
neighbor.

"Ah dunno much 'bout art," replied the
redneck, "but Ah just bought me an original
Michaelangelo for $200. It's one of the few he
ever done in ballpoint!"

* * *

151

Hinton and Crowley were having themselves a Schlitz. "My Uncle Reuben fell asleep in the bathtub with the water running," said Hinton.

"Did the bathtub overflow?" asked Crowley.

"Naw," said the redneck. "Uncle Reuben sleeps with his mouth open."

* * *

The sound of the crash was shattering and the wreckage scattered all over Hattiesburg when Yancey, racing to beat the train to the crossing, hit the 26th car.

* * *

Two Tennessee teenagers, Joe Bob and Jimmy Lee, on a bicycle-built-for-two, had a tough time getting up a steep hill.

"Ah didn't think we'd ever make it to the top," said Joe Bob.

"Yeah," said Jimmy Lee, "and it's a good thing Ah kept the brakes on, or we'd a rolled right back down."

* * *

Did you ever see a country boy in New York whistle for a cab?

He puts two fingers in his mouth and hollers, "Taxi!"

* * *

Cullman decided to attend Christmas Fundamentalist Services. He sat down with a group singing carols.

"Leon! Leon!" he sang.

The man next to Cullman nudged him. "Yew Beetlehead! Turn yore book over," he whispered. "It's Noel, Noel!"

*   *   *

Did you hear about the country boy who was so dumb he thought a Castro convertible was a Cuban bisexual?

*   *   *

Polk and Bowen were driving along South Carolina Highway 21 when suddenly Polk pulled the pick-up over to the side of the road.

"Ah don't think mah directional signals is a workin'," said Polk. "Go stand in back of the truck and tell me."

"Okay," said Bowen, getting out and walking to the rear of the vehicle. He stood silent for a few moments until finally the driver shouted: "What's happenin'?"

"They're workin' . . . they're not workin' . . . they're workin' . . . they're not workin' . . ."

*   *   *

Did you hear about the country boy who took out of the library a book called *How To Hug*, only to discover it was Volume Ten of the Encyclopedia?

*   *   *

Young Jamie decided to try out for his high school baseball team. He arrived at the practice field carrying his glove and spikes.

The coach approached him and said, "Okay. Name yore best playin' position!"

"Sorta stooped over like this," answered the country boy.

Dilmer, six-foot three, 280 pounds, was thrown from his seat when the Southern Railway train he was riding was derailed. The giant redneck flew a dozen feet through the air before he hit headfirst against a steel partition. For a moment Dilmer lay dazed, rubbing his head. The conductor kneeled down beside him.

"Don't move," said the conductor. "We called an ambulance!"

"Naw," said the Redneck, getting to his feet. "Ah ain't hurt bad. That steel wall musta broke mah fall."

* * *

Howell and Calvert were sitting in a tavern drinking Blatz. "Say," said Howell, "do yew think Bo Derek is her real name?"

Calvert thought for a minute and then answered, "Do Ah think whose real name is Bo Derek?"

* * *

"Yew little bastard!" shouted an irate woman from her backyard. "Ah'll teach yew to throw rocks at my dog!"

"Thank yew, m'am," said young Clyde. "Ah could use a few lessons!"

* * *

WORLD'S THINNEST BOOK

History of Redneck Culture

* * *

Chester: Yew told me if'n Ah rubbed grease on mah chest, Ah'd get tall like yew but it didn't work.

Brother: What'd yew use?

Chester: Crisco.

Brother: Yew lunkhead! That's shortenin'!

*   *   *

Did you hear about the redneck who thought Menstrual Cycles were put out by the Honda people?

*   *   *

Calvin, Emmett and Wilton were soaking up some suds in the Silver Dollar Saloon.

"Hey," asked Calvin, "what's yore favorite holiday?"

"Easter," answered Emmett. "Yew have turkey, and dressin' and sweet potatas."

"Yer all mixed up," said Wilton. "Mah favorite holiday is also Easter. But that's when yew put up a tree with balls and decorations on it and yew give presents."

"Ye both wrong!" said Calvin, "Easter is when Christ died. They buried him in a cave. Then three days later he came out. He done saw his shadow and went right back in!"

*   *   *

How many rednecks does it take to change a light bulb?

None. Rednecks are not afraid of the dark.

*   *   *

*　　*　　*

What do you call five KKK rednecks armed with switchblades in a dark alley?
Gentlemen.

*　　*　　*

Elmore walked into his favorite truck stop cafe and said to the owner, "Hey, Roy, you wanna take a chance on a raffle?"

"Whadaya win?" asked the owner.

"$1,000,000!" said the redneck. "You collect a dollar a year for a million years."

"How much are they?"

"Ten cents! Two for a quarter. Three for a half dollar!"

*　　*　　*

Monroe made the high school football team. One Monday afternoon the coach noticed that his socks were filthy.

"Hey," said the coach, "yew gotta put on a clean pair of socks every day before we go out for practice!"

By Friday, Monroe couldn't get his shoes on.

*　　*　　*

Did you hear about the redneck high school fullback who explained to the doctor that he had contracted VD during a wet dream?

*　　*　　*

*   *   *

Olan, a Winston-Salem tobacco grower was on his first trip to Cleveland. A taxi driver took him to an out-of-the-way whorehouse. Olan couldn't get over how polite the girls were, calling their mother, "Madam."

Next morning, he got dressed and was about to leave. "What about money?" asked the girl.

"No, thanks, M'am!" said the farm boy. "Yew've been more than kind already."

*   *   *

How do you become a redneck horticulturist?

Put a flowerpot on the back porch.

*   *   *

Lester and Willard were having a Coors in a highway road stop. They spotted two guys at the end of the bar.

"Hey," said Lester, "Ah'm goin' down and ask them fellas what they think of rednecks!"

He shuffled up to the two men and said, "Say, everybody tells jokes about rednecks and makes fun of us. Whada yawl think a rednecks?"

One of the men gave Lester the finger. The middle finger.

Lester returned to his drinking buddy. "Well?" asked Willard. "Whada they think a rednecks?"

"We're still number one!"

*   *   *

Now that the Mississippi River has been completely contaminated, what will be done with it?

It will re-open next spring as a redneck health spa.

What did the redneck say when he saw the female gorilla?

"Mama, *darlin'*!"

* * *

Did you hear about the puzzle manufacturer who has just come out with a one-piece jigsaw puzzle for rednecks?

* * *

Jasper and Newton were walking through the outskirts of Savannah when they spotted a human head lying in the road. Jasper picked up the head and held it high in the air to see better.

"Gollee," cried Jasper, "that looks like J.D. Bibb."

"Naw!" said the other redneck, "Ole J.D. was a much shorter guy!"

* * *

What do they call the first redneck who ever took a bath?

Ring Leader.

* * *

Young Bradley arrived at his date's house wearing a shirt that had water dripping from it.

"Watch yew doin'?" asked his girlfriend. "How come yore shirt is soakin' wet?"

"Well," said the redneck, "it said on the label: Wash and Wear!"

* * *

SOUTHERN GENTLEMAN
A redneck with money in the bank

* * *

Cole was walking down the road, and he ran into Hoskins. "Howdy, Cole," said Hoskins. "How's everythin' up yore way?"

Cole shook his head. "Not real good," he replied. "My daughter has took down with typhoid fever, and the old woman's dying of pneumonia. Ah shore got a peck o' trouble."

"Ah'm mighty sorry," said Hoskins. "Ah don't know nothin' about typhoid fever, and there ain't no pneumonia in our family neither. But when it comes to pecker trouble, Ah sure can sympathize with yew!"

* * *

Smithers owned a mule and asked a veterinarian to prescribe a drastic remedy for his sick, lazy critter. The vet gave him an enormous pill, promising, "This will cure him—or kill him."

"How'll Ah git him to swallow it?" asked the farmer.

"Put it in a tube," advised the vet, "and blow it into the mule's mouth."

Next day Smithers was back, looking mighty peaked. "What happened to you?" asked the vet.

"That damn mule blew first," replied the redneck.

* * *

Did you hear about the Florida redneck who thought that ping pong was a Chinese venereal disease?

$*$ $*$ $*$

Duayne met pretty Dovie Jewell from Birmingham at a Tuscaloosa ballroom. They danced almost every dance together. When the evening was over Duayne asked if he could see her next time he was in Birmingham.

"Yes," replied Dovie Jewell.

He took out a pad and pen and asked, "What's your phone number?"

"CApitol 4-6173."

After a long pause, Duayne said, "How do yew make a capital 4?"

$*$ $*$ $*$

Jelks was arrested for rape. "Don't yew worry none," said the sheriff, "yew'll be treated fair. We'll put yew in a line-up with un-uniformed policemen."

They did. The sheriff brought the victim in. Jelks saw the woman, pointed to her and said, "Yeah, that's her!"

$*$ $*$ $*$

"Hey, Paw, kin Ah have five bucks to buy me a guinea pig?"

"Here's 10 bucks, go get yoreself a Mexican gal."

$*$ $*$ $*$

"Ain't that just dumb to put shoe polish in collapsible tubes?" said Terrell.

"Why?" asked his brother.

"Yew can't fool anyone that way," said the redneck. "Ah know'd the difference the minute Ah got the stuff in my mouth."

* * *

Elmore and Baldwin shared a room on the Oklahoma college campus. One day Elmore came in and said to his roommate, "I hear there's a new case of herpes in the dorm."

"Great," said Baldwin, "I was getting real tired of 7-Up!"

* * *

In the backwoods of Kentucky how can you tell a *he* redneck from a *she* redneck?

The female redneck reaches inside her bra to count to two, and the male unzips his pants to count to one.

* * *

Delmer: How yew like the play last night over at the high school?

Farley: Ah only seed the first act, but not the second.

Delmer: Why didn't yew stay?

Farley: Ah couldn't wait that long. It sayd on the program, *'Two Years Later'*.

* * *

Why does a redneck need two hands to drink a bowl of soup?

He has to hold one hand under the fork to catch the drippings!

Young Willis had several dates with Erlene but was unable to make out. He asked his buddy Alvah what to do.

"Sheet. Jes drive her out in the country," advised Alvah, "and tell her to put out or get out!"

So Willis got Erlene into his pick-up, found a secluded spot ten miles from town and parked the truck.

"Okay," said the redneck, "now get out or Ah'll put yew out!"

*   *   *

Braxton and Hollis had jobs at a Vicksburg cotton mill. One morning the foreman came along and found Braxton reading a letter to his co-worker.

"Hey," cried the foreman, "what kind of horseplay you two guys up to?"

"Hollis got a letter from his girlfriend," explained Braxton, "but he can't read, so Ah'm readin' the letter for him."

"How come you got the cotton in your ears?"

"Hollis don't want me to hear what his girlfriend writ to him!"

*   *   *

Did you hear about the North Dakota redneck who was so dumb he thought Gatorade was welfare for crocodiles?

*   *   *

Crume was paying his first visit to Chicago. A panhandler walked up to him on Wabash Avenue and said, "Would you give me a dollar for a sandwich?"

"Ah don't know," said the redneck, "lemme see the sandwich."

*   *   *

Why do redneck hunters never indulge in sexual foreplay.

They're afraid of injuring their trigger fingers.

*   *   *

What is a nouveau riche redneck?

It is the guy on the front steps in the clean undershirt.

*   *   *

Thetchel and his girlfriend Pearl were settin' on the couch watching an old John Wayne western on TV. As Wayne rode through a pass, Thetchel said, "Ah'll bet yew a piece of ass his horse steps in a gopher hole and falls!"

"Okay," said Pearl, "you're on!"

Sure enough, the horse stumbled.

After the bet was paid in full, Thetchel said, "Ah oughta tell yew, Ah seen the movie before. That's how Ah knew."

"So did I," said the girl, "but Ah didn't think a horse'd be dumb enough to fall in the same hole twice!"

*   *   *

"Hey, Otho, where'd yew get the black eye?"

"Aw, Ah was over at mah girl's house," explained the young lover, "and we was dancin' real tight together when her father walked in!"

"So?"

"So," said the redneck, "the old guy's deaf. He couldn't hear the music!"

*　　*　　*

Mayfield, Hooley and Sisemore were sitting in a Baltimore saloon.

"There's no doubt about it," said Mayfield, "Southern pussy is the best!"

"Yeah," agreed Hooley, "Ah'd like to shack up for a long weekend with Letha, the barmaid in Louisville."

"Me!" said Mayfield, "Ah'll take two nights with Lavonne, the cocktail waitress in Nashville."

"That's nice," said Sisemore, "but Ah want Virginia Pipeline!"

"Never heard of her!" said Mayfield.

"Who is she?" asked Hooley.

"Why, she's just the greatest Southern gal of 'em all. She even made headlines in the newspaper," said Sisemore. "See, here it is on page one:

FIVE DIE LAYING
VIRGINIA PIPELINE"

*　　*　　*

Why is a redneck like a fifteen-watt light bulb?

Neither one is very bright.

*   *   *

Culley was rushed to the emergency room of the Columbus hospital. The doctor on duty was amazed to discover that Culley had scalded his testicles.

"How did it happen?" he asked.

"Ah was making me some tea," replied the redneck, "and the directions said, *Soak bag in hot water*!"

*   *   *

Pickney sat before the personnel manager in an Oregon lumber mill.

"Ah was born in Alabama," said the redneck hoping to land a job.

"What part?"

"All of me."

*   *   *

Bullock, the star college halfback was taking a math exam. They needed him desperately to play in the Arkansas game Saturday, so the professor agreed to give him an oral examination.

"All right," said the prof, "how many degrees are there in a circle?"

"Eh . . . . . . " said the redneck, "how big is that there circle?"

*   *   *

Internal Revenue Agent: What's all this?

Bellingrath: Well, yew told me to bring all my records with me and Ah did. Here's some by Ernie Ford, Roy Clark, Minnie Pearl . . .

* * *

Sauer and Tolbert went to the zoo and watched in awe as a lion let loose with a spine-tingling roar.

"Let's get out of here!" said Sauer.

"Yew go, if'n you want," said the other redneck, "but Ah'm gonna stay for the whole movie!"

* * *

Knicker walked into the poolroom flashing a large shiny pinkie ring.

"Hey," said one of his buddies, "that shore is some diamond yew got there. Is it real?"

"If it ain't," said Knicker, "Ah been cheated out of eight bucks!"

* * *

Why did the redneck drive his pick-up truck over the side of the cliff?

Because he wanted to try out his new air brakes.

* * *

Did you hear about the redneck who went to a doctor to get a hernia transplant?

*   *   *

Crumm went to a Charleston dentist complaining his gums had shriveled up and that his teeth were starting to fall out.

After examining his mouth, the dentist said, "Your mouth is real bad. Do you brush your teeth?"

"Sure Ah do!" replied Crumm. "Ever' single day."

"What do you brush them with?" asked the dentist.

"Ah use Preparation H," said the redneck.

*   *   *

Interviewer: How do you spell Mississippi?
Redneck: Do you want the river or the state?"

*   *   *

Raley had stomach trouble, so he consulted a doctor, who asked him how often he made love.

"Monday, Wednesday and Friday," he replied.

"That may be a little too much for you at your age," said the M.D. "You'll have to cut out Wednesdays!"

"Ah can't," said the redneck, "that's the only night Ah come home!"

*   *   *

Elgin showed up at the practice field to try out for the high school football team.

"What position do yew wanna play?" asked the coach.

"Quarterback!" answered Elgin.

The coach handed him a football and said, "Do yew think you can pass this ball?"

"Hell," said the redneck, "if'n Ah can swallow it, Ah can pass it!"

Jim Bob and Billy Mack walked into a Macon post office to buy stamps. They saw a poster that said: WANTED FOR RAPE with two photos of the meanest, blackest man on earth.

"See," said Jim Bob, "them niggers always get the best jobs."

*   *   *

Virgil got a job as a waiter in a Louisville motel. The second morning, during a medical convention, a group of doctors sat at his table. One of the physicians noticed that Virgil kept scratching his ass.

"Hemorrhoids?" asked the M.D.

"Sorry," said the redneck, "no substitutions on the regular breakfast."

*   *   *

Giles, the hired hand was down in the lower meadow with Farmer Drake when he carelessly cut his thumb in the mowing machine. It bled badly, and they had no first-aid kit.

"There's on'y one remedy for that there," said the old farmer. "Just go and put it in a virgin's bottom, that'll stop the bleedin' right away."

"Where'n hell yew gonna find a virgin these days?" asked Giles.

"We got us a nice, young Mexican gal just started today. Go on up to the farm house and ask her."

The senorita was a good-natured girl, and when Giles explained his problem and showed her his thumb, she dropped her panties and bent down.

After a few moments she cried out: "Hey, Señor, that ain't my bottom!"

"Ain't mah thumb, neither."

About the Author

LARRY WILDE, the world's best selling humorist, was born in Jersey City, spent two years in the U.S. Marine Corps and then graduated from the University of Miami (Fla.) He began his career in show business as a standup comedian, playing the nation's nightclubs and theaters and appearing on television commercials and sitcoms.

Mr. Wilde has appeared on the bill with such stars as Ann-Margret, Debbie Reynolds, Pat Boone and many others. He's done acting roles on *Rhoda, Sanford & Son, Mary Tyler Moore* and performed on Carson, Griffin and Douglas.

He has published two serious works on comedy technique, THE GREAT COMEDIANS and HOW THE GREAT COMEDY WRITERS CREATE LAUGHTER. Both books are recognized as the definitive works on the subject and are used as textbooks in various universities.

Mr. Wilde's 28 books are now read in every English-speaking land and have been translated into four other languages. With sales of over 7 million of his "Official" joke books have become the largest selling humor series in the history of publishing.

Larry Wilde is married to Wyoming writer Maryruth Wilde. Mrs. Wilde is the author of THE BEST OF ETHNIC HOME COOKING as well as the co-author of HOW TO TELL IF HE'S CHEATING (A Woman's Guide To Men Who Fool Around.) The Wildes live in Northern California.

Other Books by Larry Wilde

The Official Bedroom/Bathroom Joke Book
More The Official Democrat/Republican Joke Book
More The Official Smart Kids/Dumb Parents Joke Book
The Official Book of Sick Jokes
More The Official Jewish/Irish Joke Book
The *Last* Official Italian Joke Book
The Official Cat Lovers/Dog Lovers Joke Book
The Official Dirty Joke Book
The *Last* Official Polish Joke Book
The Official Golfers Joke Book
The Official Smart Kids/Dumb Parents Joke Book
The Official Religious/Not So Religious Joke Book
The Official Democrat/Republican Joke Book
More The Official Polish/Italian Joke Book
The Official Black Folks/White Folks Joke Book
The Official Virgins/Sex Maniacs Joke Book
The Official Jewish/Irish Joke Book
The Official Polish/Italian Joke Book

In hardcover

THE COMPLETE BOOK OF ETHNIC HUMOR
HOW THE GREAT COMEDY WRITERS CREATE
  LAUGHTER
THE GREAT COMEDIANS TALK ABOUT
  COMEDY

LARRY WILDE

Here's how to start your own Larry Wilde humor library!!!

HUMOR BOOKS

Looking for laughter? We guarantee you won't find any funnier or more fun books anywhere.